The Saga of the Gotlanders

Original Text, Translation, and Word Lists

Translated by
Matthew Leigh Embleton

Copyright ©2025 Matthew Leigh Embleton. All rights reserved.

The Saga of the Gotlanders

The Saga of the Gotlanders..5
Word List *(Old Gutnish to English)*...17
Word List *(English to Old Gutnish)*...36

Cover: Old Gutnish text over an outline of Gotland. Author's design.

The original Old Gutnish text is in the public domain.
This translation ©2021 Matthew Leigh Embleton
©2025 Matthew Leigh Embleton (This Edition)

Acknowledgments

I have long been fascinated by languages and history, and I am very grateful to the special people in my life who have supported and encouraged me in my work. Thank you for believing in me. You know who you are.

Special thanks to my dear friend Tove Aradala Barbrosdotter Buhe-Stam for kindly inviting me to Gotland, and for taking me on a guided tour of Gotland's beautiful historical sites. It was truly inspirational and unforgettable, and also part of the inspiration for this book.

The Translator (left) and Tove (right), Gnisvärd stone ship, Gotland, August 2019

Introduction

The Saga of the Gotlanders gives an account of how Gotland was discovered and populated, their peace treaty with the King of Sweden and annual tribute, and Olaf II of Norway's visit to Gotland, and its conversion to the Christian faith. The Gutasaga is believed to have been written in the 13th century.

What is particularly interesting about the Gutasaga is that it preserves a variety of Old Norse known as Old Gutnish. This variety of Old Norse is believed to have evolved in the 7th century along with Old East Norse and Old West Norse.

The meaning of the word 'saga' (plural: 'sǫgur' or 'sögur') translates as 'that which is said', or more widely: a 'saying', 'statement', 'story', 'tale', or 'narrative'.

The text is presented in its original Norse, with a literal word-for-word line-by-line translation, and a Modern English translation, all side-by-side. In this way, it is possible to see and feel how the Norse language worked and how it has evolved. Also included is a word list with 1,112 Norse words translated in to English, and 1,119 English words translated into Norse.

This book is designed to be of use and interest to anyone with a passion for the Old Norse or Old Icelandic language, Norse history, or languages and history in general.

The Saga of the Gotlanders

Old Gutnish	Literal	English
1	1	1
Gutland hitti fyrsti maþr þann, sum Þieluar hit.	Gotland discovered first person the, which Tjelvar named.	Gotland was first discovered by a man named Tjelvar.
Þa var Gutland so eluist, et þet dagum sank ok natum var uppi.	Then was Gotland so bewitched, that it day sank and night was raised-up.	Then Gotland was so bewitched, that it sank in the day and was raised up at night.
En þann maþr quam fyrsti eldi a land, ok siþan sank þet aldri.	Then this man brought first fire to land, and afterwards sank it never-again.	Then this man first brought fire to the land, and afterwards it never sank again.
Þissi Þieluar hafþi ann sun, sum hit Hafþi.	This Tjelvar had a son, who named Hafdi.	This Tjelvar had a son, who was named Hafdi.
En hafþa kuna hit Huitastierna.	And had wife named White-Star.	And he had a wife named White-Star.
Þaun tu bygþu fyrsti a Gutlandi.	These two settled first on Gotland.	These two were the first settlers on Gotland.
Fyrstu nat, sum þaun saman suafu, þa droymdi henni draumbr, so sum þrir ormar varin slungnir saman i barmi hennar, ok þytti henni sum þair skriþin yr barmi hennar.	First night, which they together slept, then dreamed she a-dream, thus that three snakes were coiled together in womb hers, and thought she that they slithered out-of womb hers.	The first night, when they slept together, she then dreamed a dream, that three snakes were coiled together in her womb, and she thought that they slithered out of her womb.
Þinna draum segþi han firir Hafþa, bonda sinum.	This dream told she before Hafdi, husband hers.	This dream she told to Hafdi, her husband.
Hann reþ draum þinna so:	He interpreted the-dream thus so:	He interpreted the dream thus:
"Alt ir baugum bundit. Boland al þitta varþa,	"Everything in rings bound. Inhabited-land will this become,	"Everything is bound in rings. Inhabited this land shall become,
ok faum þria syni aiga".	and get three sons have".	and we shall beget three sons".
Þaim gaf hann namn allum ofydum:	Them gave he name all unborn:	He gave them names when they were all unborn:
"Guti al Gutland aiga, Graipr al annar haita, ok Gunfiaun þriþi".	"Guti shall Gotland own, Graip shall other named, and Gunnfjaun third".	"Guti shall rule Gotland, Graip shall the other be named, and Gunnfjaun the third".

The Saga of the Gotlanders

Old Gutnish	Literal	English
Þair skiptu siþan Gutlandi i þria þriþiunga, so et Graipr, þann elzti, laut norþasta þriþiung ok Guti miþal þriþiung.	They divided afterwards Gotland into three thirds, so that Graip, the eldest, inherited northernmost third and Guti middle third.	They later divided Gotland into three thirds, so that Graip, the eldest, inherited the northernmost third, and Guti the middle third.
En Gunfiaun, þann yngsti, laut sunnarsta.	And Gunnfjaun, the youngest, inherited southernmost.	And Gunnfjaun, the youngest, inherited the southernmost.
Siþan af þissum þrim aukaþis fulk i Gutlandi so mikit um langan tima, et land elpti þaim ai alla fyþa.	Afterwards from these three increased folk in Gotland so much about long time, that land able-to them not all support.	Afterwards from these three the folk in Gotland increased so much over a long time, that the land was not able to support them all.
Þa lutaþu þair bort af landi huert þriþia þiauþ, so et alt skuldu þair aiga ok miþ sir bort hafa sum þair ufan iorþar attu.	Then cast-lots they away about the-land each third person, so that all should they own and with themselves bear keep as they above the-earth had.	Then they cast lots to send away each third person across the land, so that they should keep what they owned with thems, everything that they could carry that lay above ground.
Siþan vildu þair nauþugir bort fara, men foru innan Þorsborg ok bygþus þar firir.	Then prepared they forced away travel, but travel to Torsburgen and settled there for.	Then they prepared to be forced to travel away, and they travelled to Torsburgen and settled there.
Siþan vildi ai land þaim þula utan raku þaim bort þeþan.	Then would not land they endure but driven they away from-there.	Then the land would not endure and they were driven away from there.
Siþan foru þair bort i Faroyna ok bygþus þar firir.	Then travelled they away to Fårö and settled there for.	Then they travelled to Fårö and settled there.
Þar gatu þair ai sik uppi haldit, utan foru i aina oy viþr Aistland, sum haitir Dagaiþi, ok bygþus þar firir ok gierþu burg aina, sum enn synis.	They able-to such not themselves support keep, out travelled to one island towards Estonia, which named Dagö, and settled there for and made fortification one, which still seen.	They were not able to keep supporting themselves there, and travelled out to an island towards Estonia named Dagö, and settled there and made a fortification, which can still be seen today.
Þar gatu þair ok ai sik haldit, utan foru upp at vatni, þy sum haitir Dyna, ok upp ginum Ryzaland.	There able-to they also not themselves support, out travelled up to river, that which named Dvina, and onward through Russia.	They were also not able to support themselves there, and travelled up the river named Dvina, and onward through Russia.

The Saga of the Gotlanders

Old Gutnish	Literal	English
So fierri foru þair, et þair quamu til Griklanz.	So far travelled they, that they came to Greek-lands.	They travelled so far, that they came to the land of the Greeks.
Þar baddus þair byggias firir af grika kunungi um ny ok niþar.	There asked they settle for of Greek king about waxing-moon and waning-moon.	There they asked of the Greek emperor that they settle for the waxing moon and the waning moon.
Kunungr þann lufaþi þaim ok hugþi, et ai maira þan ann manaþr vari.	The-king this granted them and thought, that not more than one month meant.	The emperor granted them this and thought, that it did not mean more than one month.
Siþan gangnum manaþi, vildi hann þaim bort visa.	After passed month, wished he them away commanded.	After a month passed, he wished to command them away.
En þair annsuaraþu þa, et ny ok niþar vari e ok e, ok quaþu, so sir vara lufat.	But they answered then, that waxing-moon and waning-moon meant forever and always, and said, so he meant promise.	But then they answered, that the waxing moon and waning moon meant forever and always, and he had said, and so meant his promise.
Þissun þaira viþratta quam firir drytningina um siþir.	This their dispute came before the-queen about finally.	This dispute of theirs finally came before the empress.
Þa segþi han:	Then said she:	Then she said:
"Minn herra kunungr! Þu lufaþi þaim byggia um ny ok niþar.	"My Lord King! You granted them settle about waxing-moon and waning-moon.	"My Lord Emperor! You granted them to settle for the waxing moon and the waning moon.
Þa ir þet e ok e, þa matt þu ai af þaim taka".	Which means that forever and ever, then may you always of them accept".	Which means forever and ever, then may you always accept them".
So bygþus þair þar firir ok enn byggia, ok enn hafa þair sumt af varu mali.	So settled they there for and still settle, and still have they some of our language.	So they settled there and are still living there, and they still have some of our language.
Firir þan tima ok lengi eptir siþan troþu menn a hult ok a hauga, vi ok stafgarþa ok a haiþin guþ.	Prior-to that time and a-long-time after since believed people in groves and in grave-mounds, sanctuaries and sacred-sites and in heathen gods.	Prior to that time and a long time afterwards, people believed in groves and in grave mounds, sanctuaries, sacred rites, and heathen gods.
Blotaþu þair synum ok dytrum sinum ok fileþi miþ mati ok mungati.	Sacrificed they sons and daughters theirs and cattle with food and feast.	They sacrificed their sons and daughters and cattle, with food and feasting.

The Saga of the Gotlanders

Old Gutnish	Literal	English
Þet gierþu þair eptir vantro sinni.	Such did they after mistaken-beliefs theirs.	They did this in accordance with their mistaken beliefs.
Land alt hafþi sir hoystu blotan miþ fulki.	The-land all held themselves highest sacrifice with people.	The whole island held the highest sacrifice themselves.
Ellar hafþi huer þriþiungr sir.	Otherwise held each third themselves.	Otherwise each third held its own.
En smeri þing hafþu mindri blotan miþ fileþi, mati ok mungati, sum haita suþnautar, þy et þair suþu allir saman.	But smaller assembly held lesser sacrifice with cattle, food and feast, which named boiling-companions, such that they cooked all together.	But smaller assemblies held smaller sacrifices with cattle, food and feasting, they were named 'the boiling companions', because they all boiled and cooked the meat together.
2	2	2
Mangir kunungar stridu a Gutland, miþan haiþit var.	Many kings fought against Gotland, while heathen was.	Many kings fought against Gotland, while it was heathen.
Þau hieldu gutar e iemlika sigri ok ret sinum.	Though held the-Gutes always constantly victory and rights theirs.	Though the Gutes always had victory and kept their rights.
Siþan sentu gutar sendimen manga til Suiarikis, en engin þaira fikk friþ gart, fyr þan Avair Strabain af Alfa sokn.	Later sent the-Gutes messengers many to Sweden, but none of-them achieved peace made, before then Avair Strabain of Alva parish.	Later the Gutes sent many messengers to Sweden, but none of them achieved and made peace, before Avair Strabain of the parish of Alva.
Hann gierþi fyrsti friþ viþr suia kunung.	He made first peace with Swedish king.	He was the first to make peace with the Swedish king.
Þa en gutar hann til baþu at fara, þa suaraþi hann:	Then when the-Gutes him to requested to travel, then answered he:	When the Gutes requested to him to travel, he answered:
"Mik vitin ir nu faigastan ok fallastan.	"I know you now doomed and ill-fated.	"You know that I am doomed and ill-fated.
Giefin þa mir, en ir vilin, et iek fari innan slikan vaþa, þry vereldi:	Grant then to-me, if you intend, that I journey to such danger, three wergilds:	If you intend me to make such a dangerous journey, then grant me three wergilds:
att mir sielfum, annat burnum syni minum, ok þriþia kunu".	one I myself, another born son mine, and third wife".	One for myself, one for my born son, and a third for my wife".

8

The Saga of the Gotlanders

Old Gutnish	Literal	English
Þy et hann var snieldr ok fielkunnugr, so sum sagur af ganga, gikk hann a staggaþan ret viþr suia kunung.	Such that he was wise and skilled, so as the-story of goes, entered he into binding treaty with the-Swedish king.	He was such a wise and skilled man, as the legend goes, and he entered into a binding treaty with the Swedish king.
Siextigi marka silfs um ar huert, þet ir skattr guta, so et Suiarikis kunungr hafi fiauratigi markr silfs af þaim siextigi, en ierl hafi tiugu markr silfs.	Sixty marks silver over each year, which was tribute the-Gutes, so that Sweden king kept forty marks silver of the sixty, but earl had twenty marks silver.	Sixty marks of silver each year was the Gutes' tribute, so the king of Sweden kept forty marks of silver of the sixty, but the earl had twenty marks of silver.
Þinna staþga gierþi hann miþ lanz raþi, fyr en hann haiman fori.	This statute made he with land council, before when he from-home travelled.	He made this statute with the land council, before he travelled from home.
So gingu gutar sielfs viliandi undir suia kunung, þy et þair mattin frir ok frelsir sykia Suiariki i huerium staþ utan tull ok allar utgiftir.	So passed Gotland themselves willingly submitting-to Swedish king, such that they may free and unhindered travel Sweden in every place without toll and all charges.	And so it passed that the Gotlanders themselves willingly submitted to the Swedish king, so that they may freely travel unhindered to Sweden in every place without any toll or charges.
So aigu ok suiar sykia Gutland firir utan kornband ellar annur forbuþ.	So had-the-right also the-Swedish travel-to Gotland for without corn-prohibition or other prohibitions.	And so the Swedish had the right to travel to Gotland without any ban on the trade of corn or any other prohibitions.
Hegnan ok hielp skuldi kunungr gutum at vaita, en þair viþr þorftin ok kallaþin.	Protection and help should the-king Gotland to give, if they with needed and called-for.	The king should give protection and help to Gotland, if they needed it and requested it.
Sendimen al ok kunungr ok ierl samulaiþ a gutnalþing senda ok lata þar taka skatt sin.	Messengers should also the-king and the-jarl likewise to assembly send and arrange there to-take tribute theirs.	The king and the earl were to send messengers to the Gutes' assembly where they could collect their tribute.
Þair sendi- buþar aigu friþ lysa gutum alla steþi til sykia yfir haf, sum Upsala kunungi til hoyrir, ok so þair, sum þan vegin aigu hinget sykia.	The sending-command shall peace proclaim Gotlanders all places to travel over sea, which Uppsala king to belonged, and so they, who then way right here travel.	The messengers were to proclaim peace peace to travel overseas, which belonged to the king of Uppsala, and so they had the right to travel to Gotland.
Eptir þet siþan quam helgi Olafr kunungr flyandi af Norvegi miþ skipum ok legþis i hamn, þa sum kallar Akrgarn.	After that since came holy Olaf the-king in-flight from Norway with ship and lay into harbour, that which called Akergarn.	Later king Olaf the Holy on his flight from Norway by ship, put into harbour, which was called Akergarn.

The Saga of the Gotlanders

Old Gutnish	Literal	English
Þar la helgi Olafr lengi.	There lay holy Olaf long-time.	There Olaf the Holy lay a long time.
Þa for Ormika af Hainaim ok flairi rikir menn til hans miþ giefum sinum.	Then travelled Ormika of Hejnum and several influential men to him with gifts theirs.	Then Ormika of Henjum and several influential men travelled to him with their gifts.
Þann Ormika gaf hanum tolf veþru miþ andrum klenatum.	Then Ormika gave him twelve rams with other valuables.	Then Ormika gave him twelve rams with other valuables.
Þa gaf helgi Olafr kunungr hanum atr agin tua bulla ok aina braiþyxi.	Then gave saint Olaf the-king him back in-return two drinking-vessels and a battle-axe.	Then Saint Olaf the King gave him in return two drinking vessels and a battle-axe.
Þa tok Ormika viþr kristindomi eptir helga Olafs kennidomi ok gierþi sir bynahus i sama staþ, sum nu standr Akrgarna kirkia.	Then took Ormika with Christianity after saint Olaf's teaching and built himself oratory the same location, which now stands Akergarn church.	Then Ormika took with the Christian faith after Saint Olaf's teaching and built himself an oratory in the same location which now stands at Akergarn church.
Þeþan for helgi Olafr til Ierslafs i Hulmgarþi.	From-there travelled saint Olaf to Yaroslav in Holmgård.	From there Saint Olaf travelled to Yaroslav in Holmgard.
3	3	3
Þau et gutar hainir varu, þau silgdu þair miþ kaupmannaskap innan all land, baþi kristin ok haiþin.	Though the Gotlanders heathen were, they sailed they with trading-voyages to all lands, both Christian and heathen.	Although the Gotlanders were heathen, they sailed with trading voyages to all lands, both Christian and heathen.
Þa sagu kaupmenn kristna siþi i kristnum landum.	Then saw merchants Christianity custom in Christian lands.	Then the merchants saw Christian customs in Christian lands.
Þa litu sumir sik þar kristna ok fyrþu til Gutlanz presti.	Then agreed some themselves there Christianity and brought to Gotland priests.	Then some of them agreed to be baptised Christian and brought priests back to Gotland.
Botair af Akubek hit þann sum fyrsti kirkiu gierþi, i þan staþ, sum nu haitir Kulasteþar.	Botair of Akebäck named that which first church built, in that location, which now named Kulstäde.	A man named Botair of Akeback built the first church, in that location, which is now named Kulstade.
Þet vildi ai land þula utan brendu hana.	That would not the-land tolerate but burnt it.	The land would not tolerate it, and burnt it down.
Þy kallar þar enn Kulasteþar.	It was-called that still Kulstäde.	It was still called Kulstade.

The Saga of the Gotlanders

Old Gutnish	Literal	English
Þa eptir þan tima var blotan i Vi.	Then after that time was sacrifice in Vi.	After that time sacrificial feasts were held at Vi.
Þar gierþi kirkiu aþra.	There build church another.	There another church was built.
Þa samu kirkiu vildi land ok brenna.	The same church willed the-land and burnt.	The same thing happened, the people wanted to burn it down.
Þa for hann sielfr upp a kirkiu þa ok segþi:	Then went he himself up on the-church then and said:	Then he went up on the top of the church and said:
"Vilin ir brenna, þa skulin ir brenna mik miþ kirkiu þissi".	"Will you burn, this should you burn me with church this".	"If you wish to burn this church, you should burn me with it".
Hann var rikr sielfr ok rikasta manz dotur hafþi hann, sum hit Likkair snielli, boandi þar, sum kallar Stainkirkiu.	He was powerful himself and richest man daughter had he, which named Likkair wise, dwelled there, which called Stenkyrka.	He was himself a powerful and rich man, and he had a daughter, who was named Likkair the Wise, who lived there, where it is now called Stenkyrka.
Hann reþ mest um þan tima.	He ruled most about that time.	He held the most sway at that time.
Hann halp Botairi, magi sinum, ok segþi so:	He helped Botair, son-in-law his, and said so:	He helped his son-in-law Botair and spoke thus:
"Herþin ai brenna mann ella kirkiu hans, þy et han standr i Vi, firir niþan klintu".	"Let no-one burn man or church his, such that it stands in Vi, before below the-cliff".	"Let no one burn this man or his church, that stands in Vi, before the foot of the cliff".
Miþ þy fikk þaun kirkia standa obrend.	With that allowed the church stand un-burnt.	With that the church was allowed to stand un-burnt.
Han var sett þar miþ aldra helguna namni, innan þan staþ, sum nu kallar Petrs kirkiu.	It was set there with All Saints named, in that location, which now called Peter's church.	It was set their in the name of All Saints, in that location, which is now called Saint Peter's Church.
Han var fyrsti kirkia i Gutlandi, sum standa fikk.	It was the-first church in Gotland, which stands allowed.	It was the first church in Gotland which was allowed to stand.
Siþan um nequan tima eptir, lit suer hans Likkair snielli sik kristna, ok husfroyu sina, barn sin ok hiskep sin allan.	Then over some time after, arranged father-in-law his Likkair the-Wise themselves Christianity, and wife his, child his and household his all.	Then over some time after, his father-in-law and Likkair the Wise adopted Christianity themselves, and his child and whole household.

The Saga of the Gotlanders

Old Gutnish	Literal	English
Ok gierþi kirkiu i garþi sinum, þar nu kallar Stainkirkiu.	And built church in farm his, there now called Stenkyrka.	And the church built in his farm there is now called Stenkyrka.
Han var fyrsti kirkia a landi uppi i norþasta þriþiungi.	It was the-first church in land raised in northernmost third.	It was the first church raised in the land of the northernmost third.
Siþan gutar sagu kristna manna siþi, þa lydu þair Guz buþi ok lerþra manna kennu.	Afterwards Gotlanders saw Christian people customs, then obey they God's command and learned people teachings.	Afterwards Gotlanders saw the customs of Christian people, then they obeyed God's command and the people learned his teachings.
Toku þa almennilika viþr kristindomi miþ sielfs vilia sinum utan þuang, so et engin þuang þaim til kristnur.	Took then generally with Christianity with themselves will theirs without force, so that no-one forced that to Christianity.	Then the people generally adopted Christianity themselves of their own free will and without force, so that no one had forced them to Christianity.
Siþan en menn orþu almennilika kristnir, þa gierþis kirkia annur a landi i Atlingabo.	Afterwards when people became generally Christianity, then built church another in land of Atlingbo.	Afterwards when people had generally accepted Christianity, then a church was built in another land.
Han var fyrsti i miþal-þriþiungi.	It was the-first in middle-third.	It was the first in the middle-third.
Siþan varþ þriþi gar a landi i Farþaim i sunnarsta þriþiungi.	Afterwards was third built in land in Fardhem in southern-most third.	Afterwards a third was built in the land in Fardhem in the southern-most third.
Af þaim briskaþus kirkiur allar i Gutlandi, þy et menn gierþu sir kirkiur at mairu maki.	About them spread churches everywhere in Gotland, such that people built their churches for greater convenience.	Churches spread about them everywhere in Gotland, such that people built churches for their own convenience.
Fyr en Gutland toki steþilika viþr nekrum biskupi, þa quamu biskupar til Gutlanz, pilagrimar til helga lanz Ierusalem ok þeþan haim foru.	Before that Gotland took permanent with some bishop, then came bishops to Gotland, pilgrims to holy land Jerusalem and from-there home travelled.	Before Gotland took a permanent bishop, then bishops came to Gotland, pilgrims to the holy land Jerusalem and travelling home.
Þan tima var vegr oystra um Ryzaland ok Grikland fara til Ierusalem.	That time was route eastwards about Russia and Greek lands travelling to Jerusalem.	At that time the eastward route was through Russia and the Greek lands travelling to Jerusalem.

The Saga of the Gotlanders

Old Gutnish	Literal	English
Þair vigþu fyrsti kirkiur ok kirkiugarþa, miþ byn þaira, sum giera litu kirkiur.	They consecrated first churches and graveyards, with request theirs, which built had churches.	First they consecrated churches and graveyards, at the request of those who had built the churches.
Siþan en gutar vendus viþr kristindom, þa sentu þair sendibuþa til hoygsta biskups i Leonkopungi, þy et hann var þaim nestr, so et miþ steddum ret quami hann til Gutlanz þan reþskep giera miþ þaim forskielum, et biskupr vildi kuma af Leonkopungi þriþia huert ar til Gutlanz miþ tolf mannum sinum, sum hanum skuldin fylgia um land alt miþ bonda hestum, so mangum ok ai flairum.	Afterwards when the-Gutes accustomed with Christianity, then sent they messengers to highest bishop in Linköping, such that he was to-them nearest, so that with confirming statute come he to Gotland then support make with them conditions, that bishop would come from Linköping third every year to Gotland with twelve men his, who him should follow about land all with farmers horses, so many and not more.	Afterwards when the Gutes had become accustomed to Christianity, they then sent messengers to the highest bishop in Linköping, as he was nearest to them, that confirmed by statute he was to come to Gotland to give support, with the condition that the bishop would come from Linköping every third year, with twelve of his men, who should follow him about the land on farmers' horses, and not more.
So a biskupr um Gutland fara til kirkiu vigsla ok gingerþa sinna taka:	Thus the bishop about Gotland travel to church consecrate and payment his take:	Thus the bishop travelled about Gorland to consecrate churches and take his payment:
þry borþ ok ai maira at kirkiu vigsl huerri, miþ þrim markum; at alteris vigsl att borþ, miþ tolf oyrum, en alteri ainsamt skal vigias; þa en baþi iru ovigþ, alteri ok kirkia saman, þa skulu baþi vigias firir þry borþ ok þriar markr penninga.	Three meals and not more for church consecration each, with three marks; the altar consecration one meal, with twelve 'örar', if altar alone shall-be consecrated; then if both are unconsecrated, altar and church together, then shall both consecrated for three meals and three mark coins.	Three meals and not more for each church consecration, with three marks, the mere consecration of an altar shall be paid for with one meal and twelve 'örar', if the altar alone shall be consecrated; but if both are unconsecrated, altar and church together, then both shall be consecrated for three meals and three mark coins.
Af presti andrum huerium a biskupr gingerþ taka, um tilquemda siþ, þry borþ ok ai maira.	From priest second every the bishop payment takes, about visit payment, three meals and not more.	From every second priest the bishop takes payment, for his visit, three meals and not more.
Af andrum huerium presti, sum ai gierþi gingerþ a þy ari, taki biskupr af huerium lausn, so sum kirkiur iru til skuraþar.	From other every priest, which not paid payment in that year, takes the-bishop of each fee, so as church be to define.	From every other priest who did not make the payment in that year, the bishop shall take a fee, to be defined by the church.

The Saga of the Gotlanders

Old Gutnish	Literal	English
Þair sum ai gingerþ gierþu at þy bragþi, þair skulu gingerþ giera, þegar biskupr kumbr atr at þriþia ari.	That which no payment paid at that time, they shall payment make, as-soon-as the-bishop comes back at third year.	Those who did not make a payment at that time, shall make a payment, as soon as the bishop comes back on the third year.
En hinir aigu loysa, sum fyrra bragþi gingerþ gierþu.	And the-other have-to pay, which previous time payment paid.	And the others are to pay, who did not make the payment the previous time.
Kunnu dailur varþa, sum biskupr a dyma, þaar skulu lendas i sama þriþiungi, þy et þair menn vita mest af sannundum, sum þar nest boa.	May dispute occur, that bishop to deem, they shall resolve in the-same third, such that the people know most about the-truth, which there nearest settle.	If a dispute may occur, which the bhsiop will judge, they shall resolve it in the same third, as the people know the truth most, who live nearest.
Varþr ai þar þaun daila lent, þa skal han skiautas til aldra manna samtalan ok ai af þriþiungi i annan.	Becomes not there then dispute resolved, then shall he refer for all men consideration and not by third in another.	If the dispute becomes unresolved, then he shall refer to all men for consideration, and not by another third.
Kunnu hetningar eþa dailumal varþa, sum biskupi til hoyra at retta, þa a hier biþa biskups quemdar ok ai yfir fara, utan þuang reki til ok mikil synd sei, et ai ma proastr loysa.	Should disputes otherwise dispute occur, which the-bishop to hear that judge, then at here wait bishop's arrival and not over travel, unless necessity drives to and much sin be, that not may rural-dean absolution.	Should further disputes occur, which the bishop shall judge, then they shall await the bishop's arrival and not travel over the sea, unless driven by necessity or if it be a great sin that a rural dean may not grant absolution.
Þa skal yfir fara millan Valborga messur ok helguna messur, en ai þar eptir um vintrtima til Valborga messur.	Then shall over travel between Walburga mass and All-Saints mass, but not then after about winter-time to Walburga mass.	Then travel over the sea will be between Walpirgus' Day and All Saints' Day, but not after then from winter time to Walpurgis Day.
Biskups sak i Gutlandi ir ai hoygri þan þriar markr.	Episcopal charge in Gotland be not higher than three marks.	An episcopal charge in Gotland shall be no higher than three marks.
4	4	4
Siþan gutar toku sir biskup ok presti ok viþr fulkumnum kristindomi, þa toku þair ok viþr at fylgia suia kunungi i herferþ miþ siau snekkium ufan a haiþin land, ok ai ufan kristin.	After the-Gutes accepted themselves the-bishop and priest and with complete Christianity, then took they and with that join Swedish king on military-expeditions with seven warships over against heathen lands, and not over Christian.	After the Gutes themselves had accepted the bishop and priest, and Christianity completely, then they took to join the Swedish king on military expeditions with seven warships against heathen lands, but not Christian lands.

The Saga of the Gotlanders

Old Gutnish	Literal	English
So þau, et kunungr a biauþa gutum laiþing eptir vittr ok manaþar frest firir liþstemnu dag, ok þau skal liþstemnu dagr vara firir missumar ok ai siþar.	So though, that the-king to summon the-Gutes summon after winter-time and month period before mobilisation day, and then shall forces day be before midsummer and not afterwards.	So it was though, that the king summoned the Gutes after winter time and a month before mobilisation day, and then the forces shall gather before midsummer and not afterwards.
Þa ir laglika buþit, ok ai ellar.	Then be lawful summons, and not otherwise.	Then it shall be a lawful summons, and not otherwise.
Þa hafa gutar val um at fara, en þair vilia, miþ sinum snekkium ok atta vikna vist, en ai maira.	Then have the-Gutes right about to travel, if they wish, with their warships and eight weeks' provisions, but not more.	Then the Gutes have the right to travel, if they wish, with their warship with eight weeks' provisions, but not more.
Þa en gutar efla ai fylgia, þa gialdin fiauratigi marka penninga firir hueria snekkiu, ok þau at andru ari ok ai at þy sama ari, sum buþit var.	Then if the-Gutes able not follow, then fine forty mark coins for every warship, and though at second year and not that the same year, which summons was.	Then if the Gutes are not able to follow, then the fine is forty mark coins for every warship, but the following year and not the same year, when the summons was.
Þet haitir laiþingslami.	This named levy-tribute.	This is called the 'levy tribute'.
I þaim manaþi, þa skal aina viku buþkafli um fara ok þing nemnas.	In that month, then shall one week summons about travelling and assembly announce.	In that month, then shall the summons travel about to announce the assembly.
Þa en mannum sembr et laiþingr skal ut ganga, þa skal siþan halfan manaþ til ferþar boas.	Then when men agree that summoning shall out go, then shall afterwards half month to travel arm.	Then when the men agree that those summoned shall go out, then shall they afterwards have half a month to arm themselves for travel.
En siþan siau netr firir liþstemnu skulu laiþings menn garlakir vara ok byriar biþa.	But afterwards seven nights before mobilisation shall summoned men prepare be and favourable-wind await.	But after seven nights before mobilisation shall the summoned men prepare and await favourable winds.
Þa en so kann varþa, et ai kumbr byr i þairi viku, þa skulu þair enn biþa siau netr eptir liþstemnu dag.	Then if so may happen, that not comes favourable-wind in that week, then shall they still wait seven nights after mobilisation day.	Then if it may happen so, that favourable winds do not come in that week, then they shall still wait seven nights after mobilisation day.

The Saga of the Gotlanders

Old Gutnish	Literal	English
Þa en ai kumbr byr i þairi frest, þa aigu þair haim fara at saklausu, miþ þy et ai gatu þair roandi yfir haf farit utan siglandi.	Then if not comes favourable-wind in that time, then right they homewards travel that blameless, with such that not able-to they row over sea travel without sailing.	Then if favourable winds do not come in that time, then they have the right to travel home without obligation, such that they are not able to row over the sea without sailing.
Kuma laiþings buþ i minnum frestum þan manaþar, þa a ai fara utan haima sitia at saklausu.	Come summoning levy in lesser time than a-month, then have not travelled out at-home remain that blameless.	If the summoning levy comes in less time than a month, then they need not travel away from home and remain there without obligation.
Ir so et kunungr vil ai troa, et buþ quamin olaglika eþa byr hindraþi at retum frestum, þa aigu sendimenn kunungs, sum skatt taka a þy þingi, sum nest ir eptir Sankti Petrs messu, taka tolf nemdamanna aiþ, sum sendimenn kunungs nemna vilia, et þair miþ laglikum forfallum haima satin.	Be so that the-king will not believe, that summons comes unlawful or favourable-wind hinder that lawful time, then duty messengers the-king's, which tribute take have the-following assembly, which nearest be after Saint Peter's mass, take twelve chosen-men oath, as messengers the-king's announce will, that they with lawful reasons at-home stayed.	If it be so, that the king does not believe, that the summons comes unlawfully, or favourable winds hinder that lawful time, then the king's duty messengers, which take tribute at the following assembly, which is nearest to after Saint Peter's mass, take an oath from twelve chosen men, as the king's messengers will choose, that they stayed at home with lawful reason.
Engin giefs nemda aiþr i Gutlandi utan kunungs aiþr.	None given taken oaths in Gotland unless the-king's oath.	No other oaths are to be given in Gotland unless it is the king's oath.
Kann so illa at bieras, et krunaþr kunungr varþr miþ nequaru valdi bort rekinn af sinu riki, þa aigu ai gutar skatt ut giefa utan haldi hanum um þry ar.	Should such unfortunate that occur, that the-crown the-king's become with some forced away driven of his kingdom, then have not Gotlanders tribute over giving out hold he about three years.	Should such misfortune occur, that the king's crown should become forced and driven away from his kingdom, then the Gutes do not have to pay tribute but hold on to it for three years.
Ok þau aigu þair e huert ar skatt saman giera ok liggia lata, en þa ut giefa, þa en þry ar iru ut gangin, þaim sum þa raþr Suiariki.	And then have they continue each year tribute together pay and lay arrange, and then out give, then when three years be over passed, they which then rule Sweden.	And they have to continue collecting tribute each year and lay it in a trust arrangement, then hand it over, when three years has passed, to whoever rules Sweden.
Lykt bref miþ kunungs insigli skal at allum kunungs ret sendas, ok ai ypit.	Sealed letters with the-king's symbol shall that all the-king's law sent, and not opened.	All the king's letters shall be sealed and sent with the king's symbol, and not opened.

Word List (Old Gutnish to English)

Old Gutnish	English
A, a	
a	against, at, claim, have, have duty, have the right, in, into, on, on top of, own, shall, the, to
ac	and
acr	field
af	about, away from, by, concerning, from, of, out of
agin	back, in return, in-return
ai	always, continuously, ever, forever, no, no-one, not
aiga	claim, have, have duty, have the right, own, shall
aigu	claim, duty, had-the-right, have, have duty, have the right, have-to, own, right, shall
ain	one
aina	a, one
ainsambr	a, alone, one
ainsamt	alone, simultaneously
Aistland	Estonia, Estonia (a place)
aiþ	oath
aiþr	oath, oaths
akar	field
Akrgarn	Akergarn, Akergarn (a place), Åkergarn (a place)
Akrgarna	Akergarn, Akergarn (a place), Åkergarn (a place)
Akubek	Akebäck, Akebäck (a place)
Akubekkr	Akebäck (a place)
al	be, be obliged to, have to, ought to, shall, should, will
aldr	all, each, everything, everywhere, whole
aldra	all, each, everything, whole
aldri	never, never again, never-again
Alfa	Alva, Alva (a place)
alivu	eleven
all	all, each, everything, whole
alla	all, each, everything, whole
allan	all, each, everything, whole
allar	all, each, everything, everywhere, whole
allir	all, each, everything, everywhere, whole
allum	all, each, everything, everywhere, whole
almennilika	generally
alnbuga	elbow
alnbuge	elbow
alt	all, each, everything, whole
alteri	altar, both
alteris	altar
ancul	ankle
andru	and, another, following, other, second
andrum	and, another, following, other, second
ankul	ankle
ann	a, one
annan	and, another, following, other, second
annar	and, another, following, other, second
annat	and, another, following, other, second
annsuara	answer

Word List (Old Gutnish to English)

Old Gutnish	English
annsuaraþu	answer, answered
annur	and, another, following, other, second
ar	each, harvest, is, year, years
arfuþi	work
ari	harvest, harvest-year, year
arla	early
arle	early
at	at, by, concerning, for, in, in respect of, that, that , the, to, with
ata	eight
ate	eight
aþra	and, another, following, other, second
Atlingabo	Atlingbo, Atlingbo (a place)
atr	back
att	a, one
atta	eight
attu	claim, had, have, have duty, have the right, own, shall
au	and
auc	and
aug	and
auga	eye
auge	eye
auka	increase
aukaþis	increase, increased
austr	east
av	by
Avair	Avair, Avair (a name)

B, b

Old Gutnish	English
baddus	ask, asked, invite, request
bade	both
bain	bone, straight
baiþas	ask, invite, request
ban	child
band	ban, prohibition
barmbr	bosom, breast, lap, womb
barmi	bosom, breast, lap, womb
barn	child
baþi	both
baþu	ask, beg, bid, request, requested
baugr	ring
baugum	ring, rings
bei	at
bekkr	beck, stream
beþi	both
beþir	both
betr	better
betur	better
biaude	offer
biauþa	invite, offer, summon
bide	pray
biera	bear out, give birth to, happen, occur
bieras	bear out, give birth to, happen, occur
binda	bind, bound
biskup	bishop, the-bishop
biskupar	bishop, bishops
biskupi	bishop, the-bishop
biskupr	bishop, the-bishop
biskups	bishop, bishop's, Episcopal
biþa	abide, await, wait, wait for
biþia	ask, beg, bid, pray, request
blota	sacrifice
blotan	sacrifice
blotaþu	sacrifice, sacrificed
bo	property
boa	arm oneself, live, prepare, settle
boandi	arm oneself, dwelled, live, prepare, settle
boas	arm, arm oneself, live, prepare, settle
boland	inhabited land, inhabited-land, owned land

Word List (Old Gutnish to English)

Old Gutnish	English
bonda	farmer, farmers, husband
bondi	farmer, husband
borg	fortification
bort	away, bear, on one's way
borþ	meal, meal time, meals
Botair	Botair, Botair (a name)
Botairi	Botair, Botair (a name)
bragþ	point in time, time
bragþi	point in time, time
braiþyx	battle-axe
braiþyxi	battle-axe
braust	breast
bref	brief, letter, letters
brendu	burn, burnt
brenna	burn, burnt
briaust	breast
briskas	spread, spread out
briskaþus	spread, spread out
bródar	brother
brór	brother
broþir	brother
bryþlaupr	wedding
bulla	drinking vessel, drinking-vessels
bulli	drinking vessel
bundit	bind, bound, together, united
burg	fortification
burna	daughter
burnum	bear out, born, give birth to, happen, occur
buþ	bidding, command, summons
buþar	bidding, command, summons
buþi	command, invite, summon
buþit	invite, summon, summons
buþkafli	message baton, message staff, summoning baton, summoning staff, summons
bygge	build
byggia	build, live, settle
byggias	live, settle
byggja	place
bygþu	live, settle, settled
bygþus	live, settle
byn	prayer, request
bynahus	oratory
byr	favourable wind, favourable-wind, wind
byria	begin
byriar	favourable wind, favourable-wind, wind

C, c

Old Gutnish	English
came	came
cann	can
caupa	buy
ckurstain	chimney
cuma	come
cuna	woman

D, d

Old Gutnish	English
dag	day
Dagaiþi	Dagö, Dagö (a place)
dagr	day
dagum	day
daila	conflict, dispute
dailumal	conflict, dispute, matter of conflict, matter of dispute
dailur	conflict, dispute
daud	death
dauþr	death
dombr	domain
dotir	daughter
dotr	daughter
dotur	daughter

Word List (Old Gutnish to English) *Orðalisti*

Old Gutnish	English
doy	die
doya	die
draum	dream, the-dream
draumbr	a-dream, dream
drepa	kill
drepe	kill
droyma	dream
droymdi	dream, dreamed
drytning	empress, queen
drytningina	empress, queen, the-empress
dufl	gambling
dur	door
dyma	deem, deemer, judge
dýme	judge
Dyna	Dvina, Dvina (a place)
dytrum	daughter, daughters

E, e

Old Gutnish	English
e	always, continue, continuously, ever, forever, no, not
ebtir	after
efla	able, be able to
eldi	fire
eldr	fire
elivu	eleven
ella	either, or, otherwise
ellar	either, or, otherwise
elpti	able-to, be able to
eluist	bewitched
eluitskr	bewitched
elvo	eleven
elzti	eldest, old
en	and, but, however, if, that, then, when
engin	no, no one, none, no-one
engine	no, no one, none
enkia	widow
enn	but, moreover, still
eptir	according to, after, after that, after-wards, in accordance with
er	is
et	that, that, the
eþa	either, or, otherwise
ettar	after

F, f

Old Gutnish	English
fa	achieve, be allowed, get
faigastan	doomed, ill-fated
faigastr	doomed, ill-fated
faigr	doomed, ill-fated
falda	fall
faldr	doomed, ill-fated
fallastan	doomed, ill-fated
fallastr	doomed, ill-fated
falle	fall
fara	cross, go, go home, journey, leave, move, pass, travel, travelled, travelling
fari	cross, go, go home, journey, leave, move, pass, travel
farit	cross, go, go home, journey, leave, move, pass, travel
Faroy	Fårö (a place)
Faroyna	Fårö, Fårö (a place)
Farþaim	Fardhem, Fardhem (a place)
faum	achieve, be allowed, get
feire	four
ferd	trip
ferþ	journey, trip, voyage
ferþar	journey, travel, voyage
feurtan	fourteen
fiaura	four
fiauratighi	fourty
fiauratigi	forty
fielkunnugr	skilled, versatile
fierri	distance, distant, far, far away
fikk	achieve, achieved, allowed, be allowed, get

Word List (Old Gutnish to English)

Old Gutnish	English
fileþi	beast, cattle
firi	before, for
firir	because of, before, for, prior, prior-to
fisc	fish
fisk	fish
fiuhrtan	fourteen
flairi	many, more, several
flairum	many, more, several
flauge	fly
fliauga	fly
flya	flee
flyandi	flee, in-flight
folk	people
for	cross, go, go home, journey, leave, move, pass, travel, travelled
forbuþ	bidding, command, forbidding, prohibition, prohibitions, summons
forfall	causes, reasons
forfallum	causes, reasons
fori	cross, go, go home, journey, leave, move, pass, travel, travelled
forskiel	conditions, reasons
forskielum	conditions, reasons
foru	cross, go, go home, journey, leave, move, pass, travel, travelled
fran	from
frels	free, unhindered
frelsir	free, unhindered
frest	period, respite, time
frestum	period, respite, time
frir	free
friþ	freedom, peace
friþr	freedom, peace
froyia	house-woman, wife
fulc	people
fulk	folk, humans, people, population
fulki	humans, people, population
fulkumin	complete, full-come
fulkumnum	complete, full-come
furi	before, for
furir	before, for
fydum	give birth to, support
fylgia	accompany, follow, go along with, join, take part
fyr	before, before, first, for, for
fýr	before, first
fyra	bring
fýre	before, for
fyrra	first, former, previous
fyrri	first, former, previous
fyrst	first
fyrsti	first, former, previous, the-first
fyrstr	first, former, previous
fyrstu	first, former, previous
fyrþu	bring, brought
fýrti	fourty
fyþa	give birth to, support

G, g

Old Gutnish	English
gaf	gave, give
gait	goat
gamal	eldest, old, oldest
ganga	circulate, enter, go, goes, pass
gangin	circulate, enter, go, pass, passed
gangnum	circulate, enter, go, pass, passed
gar	build, built, collect, do, lend, make, pay
garlakir	prepare, prepared, ready
garlakr	prepared, ready
garn	yarn
gart	build, collect, do, lend, made, make, pay
garþi	enclosure, estate, farm, fence, yard
garþr	enclosure, estate, farm, fence, yard

Word List (Old Gutnish to English)

Old Gutnish	English
gatu	able-to, be able to, have the strength to
gera	do
gere	do
gialdin	fine, pay, pay a fine, pay out
giara	do
gief	gift
giefa	give, giving, grant, hand out, release
giefin	give, grant, hand out, release
giefs	gift, given
giefum	gift, gifts
gielda	pay, pay a fine, pay out
giera	build, built, collect, do, lend, make, pay
gierþi	build, built, collect, do, lend, made, make, paid, pay
gierþis	build, built, collect, do, lend, make, pay
gierþu	build, built, collect, did, do, lend, made, make, paid, pay
gieta	be able to, have the strength to
gikk	circulate, enter, entered, go, pass
gingerþ	payment, payment in kind, provisions, tax, tribute
gingerþa	payment in kind, provisions, tax, tribute
gingu	circulate, enter, go, pass, passed
ginum	through
góðr	good
goþr	good
Graipr	Graip, Graip (a name)
grika	Byzantine, Greek
Grikland	Byzantine Empire, Byzantine Empire (a place), Greece
Griklanz	Byzantine Empire (a place), Greece, Greek-lands
grikr	Byzantine, Greek
gúd	god
Gunfiaun	Gunfiaun (a place), Gunnfjaun
guta	Gotlander, the-Gutes
gutar	Gotland, Gotlander, Gotlanders, the-Gutes
guþ	a god, god, God (a name), gods, heathen god, idol
guti	Gotlander, Guti, Guti (a name)
Gutland	Gotland, Gotland (a place)
Gutlandi	Gotland, Gotland (a place)
Gutlanz	Gotland, Gotland (a place)
gutnalþing	assembly
gutum	Gotland, Gotlander, Gotlanders, the-Gutes
Guz	God (a name), God's

H, h

Old Gutnish	English
ha	have, she
haf	sea
hafa	have, hold, keep, retain, take
hafi	had, have, hold, keep, kept, retain, take
hafþa	had, Hafdi, Hafdi (a name), have, hold, keep, retain, take
hafþi	had, Hafdi, Hafdi (a name), have, held, hold, keep, retain, take
hafþu	have, held, hold, keep, retain, take
haga	chop, cut
hagga	chop, cut
hagge	chop, cut
hailigr	holy, saint
haim	home, homewards
haima	at home, at-home
haiman	from home, from-home
haime	at-home

Word List (Old Gutnish to English)

Old Gutnish	English
Hainaim	Hejnum, Hejnum (a place)
hainir	heathen
haita	called, named
haiþin	heathen
haiþit	heathen
haitir	called, named
halda	hold, keep, protect, retain, support
halde	hold
haldi	hold, keep, protect, retain, support
haldit	hold, keep, protect, retain, support
halfan	half
halfr	half
halp	assistance, help, helped, support
hamn	harbour
han	he, it, she, she
hana	he, it, she
hann	he, him, she
hans	he, him, his, she
hanum	he, him, she
har	hair
haþit	heathen
hau	high
haug	high
hauga	barrow, grave-mound, grave-mounds, hill, howe, tumulus
haugr	barrow, grave-mound, high, hill, howe, tumulus
haur	high
hebtir	after
heftir	after
hegnan	defence, protection
helga	holy, saint
helgi	holy, saint
helgun	all saints, saint, saints
helguna	all saints, all-saints, saint, saints
henge	hang
hengia	hang
hennar	he, hers
henni	she
her	army, military force, war, war-army
herferþ	military-expedition, military-expeditions, war-journey, war-travel, war-voyage
herra	lord
herþa	desist, leave alone, let, persist
herþin	desist, leave alone, let, persist
hestr	horse
hestum	horse, horses
hetningar	disputes, hostilities
heus	house
hialba	help
hialpa	help
hialpe	help
hiar	here
hieldu	held, hold, keep, protect, retain, support
hielp	assistance, help, support
hielpa	assistance, help, support
hier	here
hin	that-one
hindra	hinder
hindraþi	hinder
hinget	here, hither
hinir	the, the one, the other, the-other
hinn	that-one, the, the one, the other
hiskep	household, house-manner
hiskepr	household, house-manner
hit	called, named
hitta	discover, find, this
hitti	discover, discovered, find
hoygri	higher
hoygsta	highest
hoygstr	highest
hoyra	belong, hear
hoyre	hear

Word List (Old Gutnish to English)

Old Gutnish	English
hoyrir	belong, belonged
hoystu	highest
huat	what
huatki	either
huer	each, each one, every
huerghi	nothing
hueria	each, each one, every
huerium	each, each one, every
huerri	each, each one, every
huert	each, each one, every, year
hugþi	during, in, into, of, on, thought, to, within
huit	white
Huitastierna	White Star (a name), White-Star
Hulmgarþi	Holmgård, Holmgård (Novgorod) (a place)
Hulmgarþr	Holmgård (Novgorod) (a place)
hult	grove, groves
hus	house
husfroyia	housewife, woman
husfroyu	housewife, wife, woman
hut	what
hyggia	think

I, i

Old Gutnish	English
i	during, in, into, of, on, the, to, within
iac	I
iak	I
ibtir	after
iec	I
iek	I, me
iemlika	constantly
ier	be, continue, is, mean
ierl	earl, jarl, the-jarl
Ierslafr	Jaroslav (a place)
Ierslafs	Jaroslav (a place), Yaroslav
Ierusalem	Jerusalem, Jerusalem (a place)
ifir	over
iftir	after
illa	bad, evil, ill, unfortunate, unfortunately
in	in
inn	in
innan	in, into, to
insigli	authority, seal of authority, sign, symbol
iord	earth, ground
iorþ	earth, ground
iorþar	earth, ground, the-earth
ir	be, continue, in, is, mean, means, was, you, you (plural)
iru	be, continue, mean

K, k

Old Gutnish	English
kafli	baton
kalla	call, call for, name, request
kallar	call, call for, called, name, request, was-called
kallaþin	call, call for, called-for, name, request
kann	can, may, should
kara	do
karþr	yard
kaupa	buy
kaupe	buy
kaupmannaskap	trading, trading
kaup-mannaskap	trading, trading voyages, trading voyages
kaupmannaskepr	trading, trading voyages
kaupmaþr	merchant, trading-man
kaupmenn	merchants, trading-men
kaupungr	market town, town, traing town
kellare	cellar
kenna	teaching

Word List (Old Gutnish to English)

Old Gutnish	English
kennidombr	teaching, teaching domain
kennidomi	teaching, teaching domain
kennu	teaching, teachings
kialeri	cellar
kiara	do
kierua	do
kira	do
kirchia	church
kirkia	church
kirkiu	church, the-church
kirkiugarþa	churchyard, graveyard, graveyards
kirkiugarþr	churchyard, graveyard
kirkiur	church, churches
klenat	valuable
klenatum	valuable, valuables
klint	cliff
klinta	cliff
klintu	cliff, the-cliff
kom	came
kornband	corn ban, corn prohibition, corn-prohibition
koþr	good
kristin	christian
kristindom	christendom, Christianity
kristindombr	christendom
kristindomi	christendom, Christianity
kristna	christian, christianity
kristnir	christian, christianity
kristnum	christian, christianity
kristnur	christian, christianity
kruna	crown
krunaþr	crown, the-crown
Kulasteþar	Kulstäde, Kulstäde (a place)
kuma	bring, come
kumbr	bring, come, comes
kume	come
kumnum	bring, come
kuna	wife
kunna	may, should
kunnu	may, should
kunnugr	Byzantine emperor, emperor, king
kunu	wife
kunung	Byzantine emperor, emperor, king
kunungar	Byzantine emperor, emperor, king, kings
kunungi	Byzantine emperor, emperor, king
kunungr	Byzantine emperor, emperor, king, the-emperor, the-king, the-king's
kunungs	Byzantine emperor, emperor, king, the-king's
kvam	came
kýrko	church

L, l

Old Gutnish	English
la	lay, lie
ladig	spring
ladigh	spring
lag	law
lagh	law
laglika	lawful, law-like, legal
laglikr	lawful, law-like, legal
laglikum	lawful, law-like, legal
laide	lead
laiþa	lead
laiþing	summon, sea expedition, sea war
laiþingr	summon, summoning, sea expedition, sea war
laiþings	summon, summoning, sea expedition, sea war
laiþingslami	levy-tax, summon tax, sea expedition tax, sea war tax

Word List (Old Gutnish to English)

Old Gutnish	English
land	authorities, country, island, islanders, land, lands, people of the island, population, realm, the-land
landi	authorities, country, island, islanders, land, people of the island, population, realm, the-land
landum	authorities, country, island, islanders, land, lands, people of the island, population, realm
langan	long
langr	long
lanz	authorities, country, island, islanders, land, people of the island, population, realm
lata	allow, arrange, cause, leave, permit
laus	free-from, less, without
lausn	fee, fine
laut	inherit, inherited
leggia	lay
legþis	lay
lenda	resolve
lendas	resolve
lengi	a-long-time, long time, long-time
lent	resolve, resolved
Leonkopungi	Linköping, Linköping (a place)
lerþr	learned
lerþra	learned
liauta	inherit
lifa	live
liggia	lay, lie
Likkair	Likkair, Likkair (a name)
Linkaupungr	Linköping (a place)
lit	allow, arrange, arranged, cause, leave, permit
liþ	group
liþstemna	forces, group, mobilisation, summon
liþstemnu	forces, group, mobilisation, summon, summoning
litu	agreed, allow, arrange, cause, had, leave, permit
live	live
loysa	absolution, give absolution, pay, pay fee, pay fine
lufa	allow, grant, promise
lufat	allow, grant, promise
lufaþi	allow, grant, granted, promise
luge	promise
luta	cast lots
lutaþu	cast lots, cast-lots
lydu	obey
lyfta	stop
lykia	close, seal down
lykt	close, seal down, sealed
lykta	stop
lykte	stop
lysa	proclaim
lyþa	obey
lyþr	people

M, m

ma	be able to, may
maga	be able to, may
magi	son-in-law
magr	son-in-law
mair	more
maira	greater, larger, more
mairi	greater, larger, more
mairu	greater, larger, more
mak	convenience
maki	convenience
mal	case, language, matter, speech
mali	case, language, matter
manad	month

Word List (Old Gutnish to English)

Old Gutnish	English
manaþ	month
manaþar	a-month, month
manaþi	month
manaþr	month
manga	large number, many, more, several
mangir	large number, many, more, several
mangr	large number, many, more, several
mangum	large number, many, more, several
mann	man, person
manna	man, men, people, person
mannum	man, men, person
manz	man, person
margr	large number, many, more, several
mark	coin, gold, mark, silver
marka	coin, gold, mark, marks, silver
markr	coin, gold, mark, marks, silver
markum	coin, gold, mark, marks, silver
maþr	man, person
mati	food
matr	food
matt	be able to, may
mattin	be able to, may
men	but, instead
menn	man, men, people, person
messa	feast, mass
messu	feast, mass
messur	feast, mass
mest	largest, most
mestr	largest, most
meþ	with
mialc	milk
mialk	milk
mielc	milk
mik	I, me
mikil	great, large, much
mikit	great, large, much
millan	between, inbetween
millum	between
mindri	lesser, shorter
minn	mine, my
minni	lesser, shorter
minnum	lesser, shorter
minum	mine, my
mir	I, me, to-me
missumar	midsummer, summer
miþ	according to, by, in accordance with, of, on, together with, with
miþal	middle
miþal-þriþiungi	middle-third
miþan	while
miþsumar	midsummer
mungat	ale, beer, feast
mungati	ale, beer, feast

N, n

Old Gutnish	English
namn	name
namni	name, named
nat	24 hours, night
natum	24 hours, night
nautar	companion
nauþugir	forced
nauþugr	forced
nautr	companion
neir	down
nekrum	any, some
nemda	chosen, taken
nemdamanna	chosen men, chosen-men, commissioners
nemdamaþr	chosen man, commissioner
nemna	announce, decree, lay down, select
nemnas	announce, decree, lay down, select
nequan	any, some
nequar	any, some, someone
nequaru	any, some
ner	close, near, nearby
nest	closest, nearest, nearest to

Word List (Old Gutnish to English)

Old Gutnish	English
nestr	closest, nearest, nearest to
netr	nights
niþ	waning (of the moon)
niþan	below, down, low
niþar	waning (of the moon), waning-moon
niþr	down
niu	nine
no	now
nokun	someone
norþasta	northernmost
norþastr	northernmost
Norvegi	Norway, Norway (a place)
Norvegr	Norway (a place)
nu	now
ny	new, new moon, waxing, waxing moon, waxing-moon

O, o

Old Gutnish	English
oar	our
obrend	unburnt, un-burnt
oc	and
ofydum	unborn
ok	also, and, as well
Olafr	Olaf, Olaf (a name)
Olafs	Olaf (a name), Olaf's
olaglika	illegal, unlawful, un-law-like
ormar	serpent, snake, snakes
ormbr	serpent, snake
Ormika	Ormika, Ormika (a name)
orþu	arise, be, became, become, happen, occur
ou	and
ovigþ	unconsecrated, undedicated
oy	island
oyri	coin, öre, weight of silver
oyrum	coin, öre, silver-coins, weight of silver
oystra	eastwards

Ó, ó

Old Gutnish	English
óre	our

P, p

Old Gutnish	English
pa	on
penning	coin, money
penninga	coin, coins, money
Petr	Peter (a name)
Petrs	Peter (a name), Peter's
pilagrimar	pilgrim, pilgrims
pilagrimbr	pilgrim
presti	priest, priests
prestr	priest
proastr	rural dean, rural-dean

Q, q

Old Gutnish	English
quam	bring, brought, came, come
quami	bring, come
quamin	bring, come, comes
quamu	bring, came, come
quaþu	said, say
quemd	arrival
quemdar	arrival
queþa	say

R, r

Old Gutnish	English
raisa	rise
raise	rise
raku	direct, drive, driven, force
raþ	advice, counsel
raþa	carry authority, interpret, rule

Word List (Old Gutnish to English)

Old Gutnish	English
raþi	advice, council, counsel
raþr	carry authority, interpret, rule
reka	direct, drive, force
reki	direct, drive, drives, force
rekinn	direct, drive, driven, force
ret	law, lawful, proper, right, right, rights, statute
rét	right
reþ	carry authority, interpret, interpreted, right, rule, ruled
reþskeþ	support
reþskeþr	support
retr	law, lawful, proper, right, statute, treaty
retta	judge
retum	law, lawful, proper, right, statute, treaty
rikasta	richest
rikastr	richest
riki	kingdom, realm
rikir	influential, mighty, powerful
rikr	influential, mighty, powerful
roa	row
roandi	row
royra	touch
Ryzaland	Russia

S, s

Old Gutnish	English
saga	account, story, tale
sagu	saw, see
sagur	account, story, tale, the-story
sak	charge, fine, obligation
saklaus	without charge, without fine, without obligation
saklausu	blameless, blameless, sake-less, without blame
salu	soul
sama	same, the same, the-same
saman	together
sami	same, the same
samtalan	consideration
samu	same, the same
samulaiþ	likewise, similarly
sank	sank, sink
Sankti	Saint, sainted, sancti (Latin)
sanktus	sainted, sanctus (Latin)
sannund	truth
sannundum	the-truth, truth
sar	wound
satin	remain, sit, stay, stayed
scal	shall
schiauta	shoot
scogh	forest
scrifa	write
scurstain	chimney
sege	say
segia	relate, say
segþi	relate, said, say, told
sei	be, continue, mean
seine	later, then
sembr	agree, agreed, be agreed
semia	agreed, be agreed
senda	send
sendas	send, sent
sendi	sending
sendibuþa	message, messenger, messengers
sendibuþar	message, messenger
sendibuþi	message, messenger
sendimaþr	messenger, sending-man
sendimen	messengers, sending-men
sendimenn	messengers, sending-men
senn	her, his, its, their

Word List (Old Gutnish to English)   *Orþalisti*

Old Gutnish	English	Old Gutnish	English
sentu	send, sent	siþan	after, afterwards, further, later, since, then
setia	establish, lay down, set, set out	siþar	after, afterwards, further, later, since, then
sett	establish, lay down, set, set out	siþi	custom, customs, payment, tax, tribute
sia	see	siþir	custom, finally, last, lastly, payment, tax, tribute
siahs	six		
sial	soul		
siau	seven	siþr	custom, payment, tax, tribute
siauþa	boil, cook		
sidan	later, then	sitia	remain, sit, stay
sieks	six	skal	be, be obliged to, have to, ought to, shall, shall-be, should, will
siel	soul		
sielfr	himself, self		
sielfs	self, themselves		
sielfum	myself, self	skap	attitude, characteristic, manner, mind, mood, quality, undertaking
siex	six		
siextigi	sixty		
sigla	sail		
siglandi	sail, sailing		
sigldu	sail, sailed	skatt	tax, tribute
sigr	victory	skattr	tax, tribute
sigri	victory	skepr	attitude, characteristic, manner, mind, mood, quality, undertaking
sik	herself, himself, itself, themselves		
silfr	silver		
silfs	silver	skiara	cut
silgdu	sail, sailed	skiauta	refer
sin	her, his, its, see, their, theirs	skiautas	refer
		skiaute	shoot
sina	her, herself, himself, his, its, itself, their, themselves	skin	skin
		skip	ship
		skipta	divide
sinn	her, his, its, their	skiptu	divide, divided
sinna	her, his, its, their	skipum	ship
sinni	her, his, its, their, theirs	skóg	forest
		skriþa	crawl, creep
sinqua	sink	skriþin	crawl, creep, slithered
sinu	her, his, its, their	skuldi	be, be obliged to, have to, ought to, should, will
sinum	her, hers, his, its, their, theirs		
sir	he, herself, himself, itself, their, themselves	skuldin	be, be obliged to, have to, ought to, should, will
siþ	custom, payment, tax, tribute	skuldu	be, be obliged to, have to, ought to, should, will

Word List (Old Gutnish to English)

Old Gutnish	English
skulin	be, be obliged to, have to, ought to, should, will
skulu	be, be obliged to, have to, ought to, shall, should, will
skura	define, lay down, score
skuraþa	define, lay down, score
skuraþar	define, lay down, score
sla	hit
sleike	like-that
slicu	like-that
slikan	so great, such
slikr	so great, such
slingua	coil, entwine, plait
slungnir	coil, coiled, entwine, plait
smar	small
smeri	smaller
smid	smith
smier	butter
smiþr	smith
snekkia	longship, warship
snekkiu	longship, warship
snekkium	longship, warship, warships
Snelli	clever, Snielli (a name), wise
Snieldr	clever, Snielli (a name), wise
Snielli	clever, Snielli (a name), the-Wise, wise
so	as follows, in such a way, in this way, just, just so, similarly, so, such, the case, thus
socn	village
sokn	parish
sta	stand
stafgarþa	ancient site, established site, sacred-sites
stafgarþr	ancient site, established site
staggaþan	bind, binding, confirm, establish
stagba	bind, confirm, establish
stain	stone
Stainkirkia	Stenkyrka (a place)
Stainkirkiu	Stenkyrka, Stenkyrka (a place)
standa	stand, stands
standr	stand, stands
stang	pole
stanta	stand
staþ	everywhere, location, place
staþga	bind, confirm, establish, statute
staþgi	statute
steddum	confirm, confirming
stemna	meeting
steþi	everywhere, location, place, places
steþia	confirm
steþilika	confirmed, lasting, permanent
steþr	everywhere, location, place
stiela	steal
stiele	steal
stierna	star
Strabain	Strabain, Strabain (a name), straight-legs, straw-bones, straw-legs
strida	battle, fight
stridu	battle, fight, fought
stulpi	pole
suafu	sleep, slept
suara	answer
suaraþi	answer, answered
sudr	south
suer	father-in-law
sufa	sleep
Suia	Swedish, the-Swedish
Suiar	Swedish, the-Swedish
Suiariki	kingdom of the Swedes, Sweden
Suiarikis	kingdom of the Swedes, Sweden

Word List (Old Gutnish to English)

Old Gutnish	English
sum	as, as if, that, which, who
sumar	summer
sumbr	some
sumir	some
sumt	some
sun	some, son
sunnarsta	southernmost, southern-most
sunnarstr	southern-most
suþnautar	boiling-companion, boiling-companions, comrade in sacrifice, cooking-companion
suþnautr	boiling-companion, comrade in sacrifice, cooking-companion
suþr	south
suþu	boil, cook, cooked
sykia	seek, travel, travel-to, visit
synas	be seen, be visible, seen, visible
synd	sin
syni	some, son, sons
synis	be seen, be visible, seen, visible
synum	some, sons
syt	sweet
sýt	sweet

T, t

Old Gutnish	English
ta	take
taca	take
taka	accept, assume, collect, embrace, receive, take, take over, take upon oneself, takes, to-take, undertake
taki	accept, collect, embrace, receive, take, takes, undertake
til	for, thereto, to, until
tilquemd	arrival, visit, visitation
tilquemda	arrival, visit, visitation
tima	time
timi	time
tiu	ten
tiughu	twenty
tiugu	twenty
tok	accept, collect, embrace, receive, take, took, undertake
toki	accept, collect, embrace, receive, take, took, undertake
toku	accept, accepted, collect, embrace, receive, take, took, undertake
tolf	twelve
tro	belief
troa	belief, believe
troþu	believe, believed
tu	two
tua	two
tuair	two
tuldr	toll
tull	duty, excise, toll
tvair	two
tvar	two

Þ, þ

Old Gutnish	English
þa	at that time, it, now, such, that, that one, the, the following, then, they, this, when, which
þaar	it, such, that, that one, the, the following, they, which
þaim	it, such, that, that one, the, the following, them, they, to-them, which
þair	it, such, that, that one, the, the following, they, which
þaira	it, of-them, such, that, that one, the, the following, theirs, they, which

Word List (Old Gutnish to English)

Old Gutnish	English
þairi	it, such, that, that one, the, the following, they, which
þan	than, that, then
þann	it, such, that, that one, the, the following, then, they, this, which
þar	it, such, that, that one, the, the following, then, there, they, which
þau	although, besides, furthermore, however, nevertheless, stll, then, they, though
þaun	it, such, that, that one, the, the following, then, these, they, which
þegar	as-soon-as, soon
þet	it, such, that, that one, the, the following, they, this, which
þeþan	from there, from-there, thence
þiauþ	people, person
Þieluar	Tjelvar, Tjelvar (a name)
þing	assembly
þingi	assembly
þinna	this, thus
þissi	this
þissum	these, this
þissun	this
þitta	this
þorfa	have, have to, in need, need, need to
þorftin	have, have to, need, need to, needed
Þorsborg	Torsburgen, Torsburgen (a place)
þria	three
þriar	three
þrim	three
þrir	three
þriþi	third, three
þriþia	third
þriþiung	third, three
þriþiunga	third, thirds, three
þriþiungi	third, three
þriþiungr	third, three
þry	three
þu	you
þuang	force, forced, necessity
þuinga	force
þula	endure, tolerate
þy	it, such, that, that one, the, the following, the-following, they, which
þykkia	seem
þytti	seem, thought

U, u

Old Gutnish	English
u	and
uar	our
uc	and
uel	well
ufan	above, against, on, over
ufir	over
ufr	over
uir	we
um	about, around, in respect of, over, through
undir	submit, submitting-to, under
ungr	young
upp	onward, up, upp
uppi	raised, raised up, raised-up, support, up
Upsala	Gamla Uppsala (a place), Uppsala
Upsalir	Gamla Uppsala (a place)
ut	out, over
utan	but, out, unless, without
utgift	charge, expense, out-give
utgiftir	charge, charges, expense, out-give

Word List (Old Gutnish to English)

Old Gutnish	English
V, v	
vaita	give
val	choice, force, power, right
Valborga	Walburga, Walburga (a place)
vald	choice, force, power
valdi	choice, force, forced, power
vantro	ignorance, mistaken belief, mistaken-beliefs
var	be, continue, mean, was
vara	be, continue, mean, meant
vare	be
varges	nothing
vari	be, continue, mean, meant
varin	be, continue, mean, were
varþ	arise, be, become, happen, occur, was
varþa	arise, be, become, happen, occur
varþr	arise, be, become, becomes, happen, occur
varu	be, continue, mean, our, were
vaþa	danger, peril
vaþi	danger, peril
vatn	water, watercourse
vatni	river, water, watercourse
vegin	route, side, way
vegr	route, side, way
vel	well
vendus	accustom, accustomed
venia	accustom
vera	be
vereld	world
vereldi	payment, war-gold, wergild, wergilds
veþru	animal, ram, rams, yearling (a year old animal)
veþur	animal, ram, yearling (a year old animal)
Vi	holy place (a place), sanctuaries, Vi, Visby
vidur	at
vigia	consecrate, dedicate
vigias	consecrate, consecrated, dedicate
vigsl	consecration, dedication
vigsla	consecrate, consecration, dedication
vigþu	consecrate, consecrated, dedicate
vika	week
vikna	week, weeks'
viku	week
vil	intend, prepared, want, will, willing, wish
vildi	intend, prepared, want, will, willed, willing, wish, wished, would
vildu	intend, prepared, want, will, willing, wish
vili	intend, prepared, want, will, willing, wish
vilia	intend, prepared, want, will, willing, wish
viliandi	intend, prepared, want, will, willing, willingly, wish
vilin	intend, prepared, want, will, willing, wish
vintrtima	winter-time
vintrtimi	winter-time
vir	we
visa	command, commanded, send
vist	good, provisions
vita	know

Word List (Old Gutnish to English)

Old Gutnish	English
viþr	at, off, to, towards, with
viþratta	conflict, dispute
vitin	know
vittr	winter, winter-time, year

W, w

wica	week

Y, y

yfir	over
yftir	after
yngsti	youngest
ypin	open
ypit	open, opened
yptir	after
yr	out-of
yttar	after
yvar	over
yx	axe

Ý, ý

ýr	out-of

Word List (English to Old Gutnish)

English	Old Gutnish
0-9	
24 hours	nat, natum
A, a	
a	aina, ainsambr, ann, att
a god	guþ
abide	biþa
able	efla
able-to	elpti, gatu
about	af, um
above	ufan
absolution	loysa
accept	taka, taki, tok, toki, toku
accepted	toku
accompany	fylgia
according to	eptir, miþ
account	saga, sagur
accustom	vendus, venia
accustomed	vendus
achieve	fa, faum, fikk
achieved	fikk
a-dream	draumbr
advice	raþ, raþi
after	ebtir, eptir, ettar, hebtir, heftir, ibtir, iftir, siþan, siþar, yftir, yptir, yttar
after that	eptir
afterwards	siþan, siþar
after-wards	eptir
against	a, ufan
agree	sembr
agreed	litu, sembr, semia
Akebäck	Akubek
Akebäck (a place)	Akubek, Akubekkr
Akergarn	Akrgarn, Akrgarna
Akergarn (a place)	Akrgarn, Akrgarna
ale	mungat, mungati
all	aldr, aldra, all, alla, allan, allar, allir, allum, alt
all saints	helgun, helguna
allow	lata, lit, litu, lufa, lufat, lufaþi
allowed	fikk
all-saints	helguna
alone	ainsambr, ainsamt
a-long-time	lengi
also	ok
altar	alteri, alteris
although	þau
Alva	Alfa
Alva (a place)	Alfa
always	ai, e
a-month	manaþar
ancient site	stafgarþa, stafgarþr
and	ac, andru, andrum, annan, annar, annat, annur, aþra, au, auc, aug, en, oc, ok, ou, u, uc
animal	veþru, veþur
ankle	ancul, ankul
announce	nemna, nemnas
another	andru, andrum, annan, annar, annat, annur, aþra
answer	annsuara, annsuaraþu, suara, suaraþi
answered	annsuaraþu, suaraþi
any	nekrum, nequan, nequar, nequaru
arise	orþu, varþ, varþa, varþr
arm	boas
arm oneself	boa, boandi, boas
army	her
around	um
arrange	lata, lit, litu
arranged	lit
arrival	quemd, quemdar, tilquemd, tilquemda

Word List (English to Old Gutnish) — *Orþalisti*

English	Old Gutnish
as	sum
as follows	so
as if	sum
as well	ok
ask	baddus, baiþas, baþu, biþia
asked	baddus
assembly	gutnalþing, þing, þingi
assistance	halp, hielp, hielpa
as-soon-as	þegar
assume	taka
at	a, at, bei, vidur, viþr
at home	haima
at that time	þa
at-home	haima, haime
Atlingbo	Atlingabo
Atlingbo (a place)	Atlingabo
attitude	skap, skepr
authorities	land, landi, landum, lanz
authority	insigli
Avair	Avair
Avair (a name)	Avair
await	biþa
away	bort
away from	af
axe	yx

B, b

English	Old Gutnish
back	agin, atr
bad	illa
ban	band
barrow	hauga, haugr
baton	kafli
battle	strida, stridu
battle-axe	braiþyx, braiþyxi
be	al, ier, ir, iru, orþu, sei, skal, skuldi, skuldin, skuldu, skulin, skulu, var, vara, vare, vari, varin, varþ, varþa, varþr, varu, vera
be able to	efla, elpti, gatu, gieta, ma, maga, matt, mattin
be agreed	sembr, semia
be allowed	fa, faum, fikk
be obliged to	al, skal, skuldi, skuldin, skuldu, skulin, skulu
be seen	synas, synis
be visible	synas, synis
bear	bort
bear out	biera, bieras, burnum
beast	fileþi
became	orþu
because of	firir
beck	bekkr
become	orþu, varþ, varþa, varþr
becomes	Varþr
beer	mungat, mungati
before	firi, firir, furi, furir, fyr, fýr, fýre
beg	baþu, biþia
begin	byria
belief	tro, troa
believe	troa, troþu
believed	troþu
belong	hoyra, hoyrir
belonged	hoyrir
below	niþan
besides	þau
better	betr, betur
between	millan, millum
bewitched	eluist, eluitskr
bid	baþu, biþia
bidding	buþ, buþar, forbuþ
bind	binda, bundit, staggaþan, stagþa, staþga
binding	staggaþan
bishop	biskup, biskupar, biskupi, biskupr, biskups
bishops	biskupar
bishop's	biskups
blameless	saklausu
boil	siauþa, suþu
boiling-companion	suþnautar, suþnautr
boiling-companions	suþnautar
bone	bain

Word List (English to Old Gutnish)　　　　　　　　　　　　　　Orþalisti

English	Old Gutnish
born	burnum
bosom	barmbr, barmi
Botair	Botair, Botairi
Botair (a name)	Botair, Botairi
both	alteri, bade, baþi, beþi, beþir
bound	binda, bundit
breast	barmbr, barmi, braust, briaust
brief	bref
bring	fyra, fyrþu, kuma, kumbr, kumnum, quam, quami, quamin, quamu
brother	bródar, brór, broþir
brought	fyrþu, quam
build	bygge, byggia, gar, gart, giera, gierþi, gierþis, gierþu
built	gar, giera, gierþi, gierþis, gierþu
burn	brendu, brenna
burnt	brendu, brenna
but	en, enn, men, utan
butter	smier
buy	caupa, kaupa, kaupe
by	af, at, av, miþ
Byzantine	grika, grikr
Byzantine emperor	kunnugr, kunung, kunungar, kunungi, kunungr, kunungs
Byzantine Empire	Grikland
Byzantine Empire (a place)	Grikland, Griklanz

C, c

English	Old Gutnish
call	kalla, kallar, kallaþin
call for	kalla, kallar, kallaþin
called	haita, haitir, hit, kallar
called-for	kallaþin
came	came, kom, kvam, quam, quamu
can	cann, kann
carry authority	raþa, raþr, reþ
case	mal, mali
cast lots	luta, lutaþu
cast-lots	lutaþu
cattle	fileþi
cause	lata, lit, litu
causes	forfall, forfallum
cellar	kellare, kialeri
characteristic	skap, skepr
charge	sak, utgift, utgiftir
charges	utgiftir
child	ban, barn
chimney	ckurstain, scurstain
choice	val, vald, valdi
chop	haga, hagga, hagge
chosen	nemda
chosen man	nemdamaþr
chosen men	nemdamanna
chosen-men	nemdamanna
christendom	kristindom, kristindombr, kristindomi
christian	kristin, kristna, kristnir, kristnum, kristnur
Christianity	kristindom, kristindomi, kristna, kristnir, kristnum, kristnur
church	kirchia, kirkia, kirkiu, kirkiur, kýrko
churches	kirkiur
churchyard	kirkiugarþa, kirkiugarþr
circulate	ganga, gangin, gangnum, gikk, gingu
claim	a, aiga, aigu, attu
clever	Snelli, Snieldr, Snielli
cliff	klint, klinta, klintu
close	lykia, lykt, ner
closest	nest, nestr
coil	slingua, slungnir
coiled	slungnir
coin	mark, marka, markr, markum, oyri, oyrum, penning, penninga
coins	penninga
collect	gar, gart, giera, gierþi, gierþis, gierþu, taka, taki, tok, toki, toku

Word List (English to Old Gutnish) — Orþalisti

English	Old Gutnish
come	cuma, kuma, kumbr, kume, kumnum, quam, quami, quamin, quamu
comes	kumbr, quamin
command	buþ, buþar, buþi, forbuþ, visa
commanded	visa
commissioner	nemdamaþr
commissioners	nemdamanna
companion	nautar, nautr
complete	fulkumin, fulkumnum
comrade in sacrifice	suþnautar, suþnautr
concerning	af, at
conditions	forskiel, forskielum
confirm	staggaþan, stagþa, staþga, steddum, steþia
confirmed	steþilika
confirming	steddum
conflict	daila, dailumal, dailur, viþratta
consecrate	vigia, vigias, vigsla, vigþu
consecrated	vigias, vigþu
consecration	vigsl, vigsla
consideration	samtalan
constantly	iemlika
continue	e, ier, ir, iru, sei, var, vara, vari, varin, varu
continuously	ai, e
convenience	mak, maki
cook	siauþa, suþu
cooked	suþu
cooking-companion	suþnautar, suþnautr
corn ban	kornband
corn prohibition	kornband
corn-prohibition	kornband
council	raþi
counsel	raþ, raþi
country	land, landi, landum, lanz
crawl	skriþa, skriþin
creep	skriþa, skriþin
cross	fara, fari, farit, for, fori, foru
crown	kruna, krunaþr
custom	siþ, siþi, siþir, siþr
customs	siþi
cut	haga, hagga, hagge, skiara

D, d

English	Old Gutnish
Dagö	Dagaiþi
Dagö (a place)	Dagaiþi
danger	vaþa, vaþi
daughter	burna, dotir, dotr, dotur, dytrum
daughters	dytrum
day	dag, dagr, dagum
death	daud, dauþr
decree	nemna, nemnas
dedicate	vigia, vigias, vigþu
dedication	vigsl, vigsla
deem	dyma
deemer	dyma
defence	hegnan
define	skura, skuraþa, skuraþar
desist	herþa, herþin
did	gierþu
die	doy, doya
direct	raku, reka, reki, rekinn
discover	hitta, hitti
discovered	hitti
dispute	daila, dailumal, dailur, viþratta
disputes	hetningar
distance	fierri
distant	fierri
divide	skipta, skiptu
divided	skiptu
do	gar, gart, gera, gere, giara, giera, gierþi, gierþis, gierþu, kara, kiara, kierua, kira
domain	dombr
doomed	faigastan, faigastr, faigr, faldr, fallastan, fallastr
door	dur
down	neir, niþan, niþr

39

Word List (English to Old Gutnish) *Orþalisti*

English	Old Gutnish
dream	draum, draumbr, droyma, droymdi
dreamed	droymdi
drinking vessel	bulla, bulli
drinking-vessels	bulla
drive	raku, reka, reki, rekinn
driven	raku, rekinn
drives	reki
during	hugþi, i
duty	aigu, tull
Dvina	Dyna
Dvina (a place)	Dyna
dwelled	boandi

E, e

English	Old Gutnish
each	aldr, aldra, all, alla, allan, allar, allir, allum, alt, ar, huer, hueria, huerium, huerri, huert
each one	huer, hueria, huerium, huerri, huert
earl	ierl
early	arla, arle
earth	iord, iorþ, iorþar
east	austr
eastwards	oystra
eight	ata, ate, atta
either	ella, ellar, eþa, huatki
elbow	alnbuga, alnbuge
eldest	elzti, gamal
eleven	alivu, elivu, elvo
embrace	taka, taki, tok, toki, toku
emperor	kunnugr, kunung, kunungar, kunungi, kunungr, kunungs
empress	drytning, drytningina
enclosure	garþi, garþr
endure	þula
enter	ganga, gangin, gangnum, gikk, gingu
entered	gikk
entwine	slingua, slungnir
Episcopal	Biskups

English	Old Gutnish
establish	setia, sett, staggaþan, stagþa, staþga
established site	stafgarþa, stafgarþr
estate	garþi, garþr
Estonia	Aistland
Estonia (a place)	Aistland
ever	ai, e
every	huer, hueria, huerium, huerri, huert
everything	aldr, aldra, all, alla, allan, allar, allir, allum, alt
everywhere	aldr, allar, allir, allum, staþ, steþi, steþr
evil	illa
excise	tull
expense	utgift, utgiftir
eye	auga, auge

F, f

English	Old Gutnish
fall	falda, falle
far	fierri
far away	fierri
Fardhem	Farþaim
Fardhem (a place)	Farþaim
farm	garþi, garþr
farmer	bonda, bondi
farmers	bonda
Fårö	Faroyna
Fårö (a place)	Faroy, Faroyna
father-in-law	suer
favourable wind	byr, byriar
favourable-wind	byr, byriar
feast	messa, messu, messur, mungat, mungati
fee	lausn
fence	garþi, garþr
field	acr, akar
fight	strida, stridu
finally	siþir
find	hitta, hitti
fine	gialdin, lausn, sak
fire	eldi, eldr

Word List (English to Old Gutnish)   *Orþalisti*

English	Old Gutnish
first	fyr, fyrra, fyrri, fyrst, fyrsti, fyrstr, fyrstu
fish	fisc, fisk
flee	flya, flyandi
fly	flauge, fliauga
folk	fulk
follow	fylgia
following	andru, andrum, annan, annar, annat, annur, aþra
food	mati, matr
for	at, firi, firir, furi, furir, fyr, fýr, fýre, til
forbidding	forbuþ
force	raku, reka, reki, rekinn, þuang, þuinga, val, vald, valdi
forced	nauþugir, nauþugr, þuang, valdi
forces	liþstemna, liþstemnu
forest	scogh, skóg
forever	ai, e
former	fyr, fyrra, fyrri, fyrsti, fyrstr, fyrstu
fortification	borg, burg
forty	fiauratigi
fought	stridu
four	feire, fiaura
fourteen	feurtan, fiuhrtan
fourty	fiauratighi, fýrti
free	frels, frelsir, frir
freedom	friþ, friþr
free-from	laus
from	af, fran
from home	haiman
from there	þeþan
from-home	haiman
from-there	þeþan
full-come	fulkumin, fulkumnum
further	siþan, siþar
furthermore	þau

G, g

English	Old Gutnish
gambling	dufl
Gamla Uppsala (a place)	Upsala, Upsalir
gave	gaf
generally	almennilika
get	fa, faum, fikk
gift	gief, giefs, giefum
gifts	giefum
give	gaf, giefa, giefin, vaita
give absolution	loysa
give birth to	biera, bieras, burnum, fydum, fyþa
given	giefs
giving	giefa
go	fara, fari, farit, for, fori, foru, ganga, gangin, gangnum, gikk, gingu
go along with	fylgia
go home	fara, fari, farit, for, fori, foru
goat	gait
god	gúd, guþ
God (a name)	Guþ, Guz
gods	guþ
God's	Guz
goes	ganga
gold	mark, marka, markr, markum
good	gódr, goþr, koþr, vist
Gotland	gutar, Gutland, Gutlandi, Gutlanz, gutum
Gotland (a place)	Gutland, Gutlandi, Gutlanz
Gotlander	guta, gutar, guti, gutum
Gotlanders	gutar, gutum
Graip	Graipr
Graip (a name)	Graipr
grant	giefa, giefin, lufa, lufat, lufaþi
granted	lufaþi
grave-mound	hauga, haugr
grave-mounds	hauga
graveyard	kirkiugarþa, kirkiugarþr
graveyards	kirkiugarþa
great	mikil, mikit
greater	maira, mairi, mairu

Word List (English to Old Gutnish) — Orþalisti

English	Old Gutnish
Greece	Grikland, Griklanz
Greek	grika, grikr
Greek-lands	Griklanz
ground	iord, iorþ, iorþar
group	liþ, liþstemna, liþstemnu
grove	hult
groves	hult
Gunfiaun (a place)	Gunfiaun
Gunnfjaun	Gunfiaun
Guti	Guti
Guti (a name)	Guti

H, h

English	Old Gutnish
had	attu, hafi, hafþa, hafþi, litu
had-the-right	aigu
Hafdi	Hafþa, Hafþi
Hafdi (a name)	Hafþa, Hafþi
hair	har
half	halfan, halfr
hand out	giefa, giefin
hang	henge, hengia
happen	biera, bieras, burnum, orþu, varþ, varþa, varþr
harbour	hamn
harvest	ar, ari
harvest-year	ari
have	a, aiga, aigu, attu, ha, hafa, hafi, Hafþa, Hafþi, hafþu, þorfa, þorftin
have duty	a, aiga, aigu, attu
have the right	a, aiga, aigu, attu
have the strength to	gatu, gieta
have to	al, skal, skuldi, skuldin, skuldu, skulin, skulu, þorfa, þorftin
have-to	aigu
he	han, hana, hann, hans, hanum, hennar, sir
hear	hoyra, hoyre
heathen	hainir, haiþin, haiþit, haþit
heathen god	guþ
Hejnum	Hainaim
Hejnum (a place)	Hainaim
held	hafþi, hafþu, hieldu
help	halp, hialba, hialpa, hialpe, hielp, hielpa
helped	halp
her	senn, sin, sina, sinn, sinna, sinni, sinu, sinum
here	hiar, hier, hinget
hers	hennar, sinum
herself	sik, sina, sir
high	hau, haug, haugr, haur
higher	hoygri
highest	hoygsta, hoygstr, hoystu
hill	hauga, haugr
him	hann, hans, hanum
himself	sielfr, sik, sina, sir
hinder	hindra, hindraþi
his	hans, senn, sin, sina, sinn, sinna, sinni, sinu, sinum
hit	sla
hither	hinget
hold	hafa, hafi, Hafþa, Hafþi, hafþu, halda, halde, haldi, haldit, hieldu
Holmgård	Hulmgarþi
Holmgård (Novgorod) (a place)	Hulmgarþi, Hulmgarþr
holy	hailigr, helga, helgi
holy place (a place)	Vi
home	haim
homewards	haim
horse	hestr, hestum
horses	hestum
hostilities	hetningar
house	heus, hus
household	hiskep, hiskepr
house-manner	hiskep, hiskepr
housewife	husfroyia, husfroyu

Word List (English to Old Gutnish) — Orþalisti

English	Old Gutnish
house-woman	froyia
howe	hauga, haugr
however	en, þau
humans	fulk, fulki
husband	bonda, bondi

I, i

English	Old Gutnish
I	iac, iak, iec, iek, mik, mir
idol	guþ
if	en
ignorance	vantro
ill	illa
illegal	olaglika
ill-fated	faigastan, faigastr, faigr, faldr, fallastan, fallastr
in	a, at, hugþi, i, in, inn, innan, ir
in accordance with	eptir, miþ
in need	þorfa
in respect of	at, um
in return	agin
in such a way	so
in this way	so
inbetween	millan
increase	auka, aukaþis
increased	aukaþis
in-flight	flyandi
influential	rikir, rikr
inhabited land	boland
inhabited-land	boland
inherit	laut, liauta
inherited	laut
in-return	agin
instead	men
intend	vil, vildi, vildu, vili, vilia, viliandi, vilin
interpret	raþa, raþr, reþ
interpreted	reþ
into	a, hugþi, i, innan
invite	baddus, baiþas, biauþa, buþi, buþit
is	ar, er, ier, ir
island	land, landi, landum, lanz, oy
islanders	land, landi, landum, lanz
it	han, hana, þa, þaar, þaim, þair, þaira, þairi, þann, þar, þaun, þet, þy
its	senn, sin, sina, sinn, sinna, sinni, sinu, sinum
itself	sik, sina, sir

J, j

English	Old Gutnish
jarl	ierl
Jaroslav (a place)	Ierslafr, Ierslafs
Jerusalem	Ierusalem
Jerusalem (a place)	Ierusalem
join	fylgia
journey	fara, fari, farit, ferþ, ferþar, for, fori, foru
judge	dyma, dýme, retta
just	so
just so	so

K, k

English	Old Gutnish
keep	hafa, hafi, Hafþa, Hafþi, hafþu, halda, haldi, haldit, hieldu
kept	hafi
kill	drepa, drepe
king	kunnugr, kunung, kunungar, kunungi, kunungr, kunungs
kingdom	riki
kingdom of the Swedes	Suiariki, Suiarikis
kings	kunungar
know	vita, vitin
Kulstäde	Kulasteþar
Kulstäde (a place)	Kulasteþar

L, l

Word List (English to Old Gutnish) — Orþalisti

English	Old Gutnish
land	land, landi, landum, lanz
lands	land, landum
language	mal, mali
lap	barmbr, barmi
large	mikil, mikit
large number	manga, mangir, mangr, mangum, margr
larger	maira, mairi, mairu
largest	mest, mestr
last	siþir
lasting	steþilika
lastly	siþir
later	seine, sidan, siþan, siþar
law	lag, lagh, ret, retr, retum
lawful	laglika, laglikr, laglikum, ret, retr, retum
law-like	laglika, laglikr, laglikum
lay	la, leggia, legþis, liggia
lay down	nemna, nemnas, setia, sett, skura, skuraþa, skuraþar
lead	laide, laiþa
learned	lerþr, lerþra
leave	fara, fari, farit, for, fori, foru, lata, lit, litu
leave alone	herþa, herþin
legal	laglika, laglikr, laglikum
lend	gar, gart, giera, gierþi, gierþis, gierþu
less	laus
lesser	mindri, minni, minnum
let	herþa, herþin
letter	bref
letters	bref
levy-tax	laiþingslami
lie	la, liggia
like-that	sleike, slicu
likewise	samulaiþ
Likkair	Likkair
Likkair (a name)	Likkair
Linköping	Leonkopungi
Linköping (a place)	Leonkopungi, Linkaupungr
live	boa, boandi, boas, byggia, byggias, bygþu, bygþus, lifa, live
location	staþ, steþi, steþr
long	langan, langr
long time	lengi
longship	snekkia, snekkiu, snekkium
long-time	lengi
lord	herra
low	niþan

M, m

English	Old Gutnish
made	gart, gierþi, gierþu
make	gar, gart, giera, gierþi, gierþis, gierþu
man	mann, manna, mannum, manz, maþr, menn
manner	skap, skepr
many	flairi, flairum, manga, mangir, mangr, mangum, margr
mark	mark, marka, markr, markum
market town	kaupungr
marks	marka, markr, markum
mass	messa, messu, messur
matter	mal, mali
matter of conflict	dailumal
matter of dispute	dailumal
may	kann, kunna, kunnu, ma, maga, matt, mattin
me	iek, mik, mir
meal	borþ
meal time	borþ
meals	borþ

Word List (English to Old Gutnish) — Orþalisti

English	Old Gutnish
mean	ier, ir, iru, sei, var, vara, vari, varin, varu
means	ir
meant	vara, vari
meeting	stemna
men	manna, mannum, menn
merchant	kaupmaþr
merchants	kaupmenn
message	sendibuþa, sendibuþar, sendibuþi
message baton	buþkafli
message staff	buþkafli
messenger	sendibuþa, sendibuþar, sendibuþi, sendimaþr
messengers	sendibuþa, sendimen, sendimenn
middle	miþal
middle-third	miþal-þriþiungi
midsummer	missumar, miþsumar
mighty	rikir, rikr
military force	her
military-expedition	herferþ
military-expeditions	herferþ
milk	mialc, mialk, mielc
mind	skap, skepr
mine	minn, minum
mistaken belief	vantro
mistaken-beliefs	vantro
mobilisation	liþstemna, liþstemnu
money	penning, penninga
month	manad, manaþ, manaþar, manaþi, manaþr
mood	skap, skepr
more	flairi, flairum, mair, maira, mairi, mairu, manga, mangir, mangr, mangum, margr
moreover	enn
most	mest, mestr
move	fara, fari, farit, for, fori, foru
much	mikil, mikit

English	Old Gutnish
summon	laiþing, laiþingr, laiþings, liþstemna, liþstemnu
summon tax	laiþingslami
summoning	laiþingr, laiþings, liþstemnu
my	minn, minum
myself	sielfum

N, n

English	Old Gutnish
name	kalla, kallar, kallaþin, namn, namni
named	haita, haitir, hit, namni
near	ner
nearby	ner
nearest	nest, nestr
nearest to	nest, nestr
necessity	þuang
need	þorfa, þorftin
need to	þorfa, þorftin
needed	þorftin
never	aldri
never again	aldri
never-again	aldri
nevertheless	þau
new	ny
new moon	ny
night	nat, natum
nights	netr
nine	niu
no	ai, e, engin, engine
no one	engin, engine
none	engin, engine
no-one	ai, engin
northernmost	norþasta, norþastr
Norway	Norvegi
Norway (a place)	Norvegi, Norvegr
not	ai, e
nothing	huerghi, varges
now	no, nu, þa

O, o

Word List (English to Old Gutnish) — *Orþalisti*

English	Old Gutnish
oath	aiþ, aiþr
oaths	aiþr
obey	lydu, lyþa
obligation	sak
occur	biera, bieras, burnum, orþu, varþ, varþa, varþr
of	af, hugþi, i, miþ
off	viþr
offer	biaude, biauþa
of-them	þaira
Olaf	Olafr
Olaf (a name)	Olafr, Olafs
Olaf's	Olafs
old	elzti, gamal
oldest	gamal
on	a, hugþi, i, miþ, pa, ufan
on one's way	bort
on top of	a
one	ain, aina, ainsambr, ann, att
onward	upp
open	ypin, ypit
opened	ypit
or	ella, ellar, eþa
oratory	bynahus
Ormika	Ormika
Ormika (a name)	Ormika
other	andru, andrum, annan, annar, annat, annur, aþra
otherwise	ella, ellar, eþa
ought to	al, skal, skuldi, skuldin, skuldu, skulin, skulu
our	oar, óre, uar, varu
out	ut, utan
out of	af
out-give	utgift, utgiftir
out-of	yr, ýr
over	ifir, ufan, ufir, ufr, um, ut, yfir, yvar
own	a, aiga, aigu, attu
owned land	boland

Ö, ö

English	Old Gutnish
öre	oyri, oyrum

P, p

English	Old Gutnish
paid	gierþi, gierþu
parish	sokn
pass	fara, fari, farit, for, fori, foru, ganga, gangin, gangnum, gikk, gingu
passed	gangin, gangnum, gingu
pay	gar, gart, gialdin, gielda, giera, gierþi, gierþis, gierþu, loysa
pay a fine	gialdin, gielda
pay fee	loysa
pay fine	loysa
pay out	gialdin, gielda
payment	gingerþ, siþ, siþi, siþir, siþr, vereldi
payment in kind	gingerþ, gingerþa
peace	friþ, friþr
people	folk, fulc, fulk, fulki, lyþr, manna, menn, þiauþ
people of the island	land, landi, landum, lanz
peril	vaþa, vaþi
period	frest, frestum
permanent	steþilika
permit	lata, lit, litu
persist	herþa, herþin
person	mann, manna, mannum, manz, maþr, menn, þiauþ
Peter (a name)	Petr, Petrs
Peter's	Petrs
pilgrim	pilagrimar, pilagrimbr
pilgrims	pilagrimar
place	byggja, staþ, steþi, steþr
places	steþi
plait	slingua, slungnir
point in time	bragþ, bragþi

Word List (English to Old Gutnish)   *Orþalisti*

English	Old Gutnish	English	Old Gutnish
pole	stang, stulpi	reasons	forfall, forfallum, forskiel, forskielum
population	fulk, fulki, land, landi, landum, lanz	receive	taka, taki, tok, toki, toku
power	val, vald, valdi	refer	skiauta, skiautas
powerful	rikir, rikr	relate	segia, segþi
pray	bide, biþia	release	giefa, giefin
prayer	byn	remain	satin, sitia
prepare	boa, boandi, boas, garlakir	request	baddus, baiþas, baþu, biþia, byn, kalla, kallar, kallaþin
prepared	garlakir, garlakr, vil, vildi, vildu, vili, vilia, viliandi, vilin	requested	baþu
previous	fyr, fyrra, fyrri, fyrsti, fyrstr, fyrstu	resolve	lenda, lendas, lent
		resolved	lent
priest	presti, prestr	respite	frest, frestum
priests	presti	retain	hafa, hafi, Hafþa, Hafþi, hafþu, halda, haldi, haldit, hieldu
prior	firir		
prior-to	Firir		
proclaim	lysa	richest	rikasta, rikastr
prohibition	band, forbuþ	right	aigu, ret, rét, reth, retr, retum, val
prohibitions	forbuþ		
promise	lufa, lufat, lufaþi, luge	rights	ret
proper	ret, retr, retum	ring	baugr, baugum
property	bo	rings	baugum
protect	halda, haldi, haldit, hieldu	rise	raisa, raise
		river	vatni
protection	hegnan	route	vegin, vegr
provisions	gingerþ, gingerþa, vist	row	roa, roandi
		rule	raþa, raþr, reþ
		ruled	reþ
		rural dean	proastr
		rural-dean	proastr
		Russia	Ryzaland

Q, q

quality	skap, skepr		
queen	drytning, drytningina		

S, s

R, r

English	Old Gutnish
sacred-sites	stafgarþa
sacrifice	blota, blotan, blotaþu
sacrificed	Blotaþu
said	quaþu, segþi
sail	sigla, siglandi, sigldu, silgdu
sailed	sigldu, silgdu
sailing	siglandi

English	Old Gutnish
raised	uppi
raised up	uppi
raised-up	uppi
ram	veþru, veþur
rams	veþru
ready	garlakir, garlakr
realm	land, landi, landum, lanz, riki

Word List (English to Old Gutnish) Orþalisti

English	Old Gutnish	English	Old Gutnish
saint	hailigr, helga, helgi, helgun, helguna, Sankti	settled	bygþu
		seven	siau
		several	flairi, flairum, manga, mangir, mangr, mangum, margr
sainted	sankti, sanktus		
saints	helgun, helguna	shall	a, aiga, aigu, al, attu, scal, skal, skulu
sake-less	saklausu		
same	sama, sami, samu	shall-be	skal
sancti (Latin)	sankti	she	han, hana, hann, hans, hanum, henni
sanctuaries	vi		
sanctus (Latin)	sanktus	she	ha, han
sank	sank	ship	skip, skipum
saw	sagu	shoot	schiauta, skiaute
say	quaþu, queþa, sege, segia, segþi	shorter	mindri, minni, minnum
		should	al, kann, kunna, kunnu, skal, skuldi, skuldin, skuldu, skulin, skulu
score	skura, skuraþa, skuraþar		
sea	haf		
sea expedition	laiþing, laiþingr, laiþings	side	vegin, vegr
		sign	insigli
sea expedition tax	laiþingslami	silver	mark, marka, markr, markum, silfr, silfs
sea war	laiþing, laiþingr, laiþings		
		silver-coins	oyrum
sea war tax	laiþingslami	similarly	samulaiþ, so
seal down	lykia, lykt	simultaneously	ainsamt
seal of authority	insigli	sin	synd
sealed	Lykt	since	siþan, siþar
second	andru, andrum, annan, annar, annat, annur, aþra	sink	sank, sinqua
		sit	satin, sitia
see	sagu, sia, sin	six	siahs, sieks, siex
seek	sykia	sixty	siextigi
seem	þykkia, þytti	skilled	fielkunnugr
seen	synas, synis	skin	skin
select	nemna, nemnas	sleep	suafu, sufa
self	sielfr, sielfs, sielfum	slept	suafu
send	senda, sendas, sentu, visa	slithered	skriþin
		small	smar
sending	sendi	smaller	smeri
sending-man	sendimaþr	smith	smid, smiþr
sending-men	sendimen, sendimenn	snake	ormar, ormbr
sent	sendas, sentu	snakes	ormar
serpent	ormar, ormbr	Snielli (a name)	Snelli, Snieldr, Snielli
set	setia, sett	so	so
set out	setia, sett	so great	slikan, slikr
settle	boa, boandi, boas, byggia, byggias, bygþu, bygþus		

Word List (English to Old Gutnish) *Orþalisti*

English	Old Gutnish
some	nekrum, nequan, nequar, nequaru, sumbr, sumir, sumt, sun, syni, synum
someone	nequar, nokun
son	sun, syni
son-in-law	magi, magr
sons	syni, synum
soon	þegar
soul	salu, sial, siel
south	sudr, suþr
southernmost	sunnarsta
southern-most	sunnarsta, sunnarstr
speech	mal
spread	briskas, briskaþus
spread out	briskas, briskaþus
spring	ladig, ladigh
stand	sta, standa, standr, stanta
stands	standa, standr
star	stierna
statute	ret, retr, retum, staþga, staþgi
stay	satin, sitia
stayed	satin
steal	stiela, stiele
Stenkyrka	Stainkirkiu
Stenkyrka (a place)	Stainkirkia, Stainkirkiu
still	enn
stll	þau
stone	stain
stop	lyfta, lykta, lykte
story	saga, sagur
Strabain	Strabain
Strabain (a name)	Strabain
straight	bain
straight-legs	Strabain
straw-bones	Strabain
straw-legs	Strabain
stream	bekkr
submit	undir
submitting-to	undir
such	slikan, slikr, so, þa, þaar, þaim, þair, þaira, þairi, þann, þar, þaun, þet, þy
summer	missumar, sumar
summon	biauþa, buþi, buþit
summoning baton	buþkafli
summoning staff	buþkafli
summons	buþ, buþar, buþit, buþkafli, forbuþ
support	fydum, fyþa, halda, haldi, haldit, halp, hieldu, hielp, hielpa, reþskep, reþskepr, uppi
Sweden	Suiariki, Suiarikis
Swedish	Suia, Suiar
sweet	syt, sýt
symbol	insigli

T, t

English	Old Gutnish
take	hafa, hafi, Hafþa, Hafþi, hafþu, ta, taca, taka, taki, tok, toki, toku
take over	taka
take part	fylgia
take upon oneself	taka
taken	nemda
takes	taka, taki
tale	saga, sagur
tax	gingerþ, gingerþa, siþ, siþi, siþir, siþr, skatt, skattr
teaching	kenna, kennidombr, kennidomi, kennu
teaching domain	kennidombr, kennidomi
teachings	kennu
ten	tiu
than	þan
that	at, en, et, sum, þa, þaar, þaim, þair, þaira, þairi, þan, þann, þar, þaun, þet, þy
that	at, et
that one	þa, þaar, þaim, þair, þaira, þairi, þann, þar, þaun, þet, þy
that-one	hin, hinn

49

Word List (English to Old Gutnish)   *Orþalisti*

English	Old Gutnish
the	a, at, et, hinir, hinn, i, Þa, þaar, þaim, þair, þaira, þairi, þann, þar, þaun, þet, þy
the case	so
the following	þa, þaar, þaim, þair, þaira, þairi, þann, þar, þaun, þet, þy
the one	hinir, hinn
the other	hinir, hinn
the same	sama, sami, samu
the-bishop	biskup, biskupi, biskupr
the-church	kirkiu
the-cliff	klintu
the-crown	krunaþr
the-dream	draum
the-earth	iorþar
the-emperor	Kunungr
the-empress	drytningina
the-first	fyrsti
the-following	þy
the-Gutes	guta, gutar, gutum
their	senn, sin, sina, sinn, sinna, sinni, sinu, sinum, sir
theirs	sin, sinni, sinum, þaira
the-jarl	ierl
the-king	kunungr
the-king's	kunungr, kunungs
the-land	Land, landi
them	þaim
themselves	sielfs, sik, sina, sir
then	en, seine, sidan, siþan, siþar, þa, þan, Þann, þar, þau, þaun
thence	þeþan
the-other	hinir
there	þar
thereto	til
the-same	sama
these	þaun, þissum
the-story	sagur
the-Swedish	suia, suiar
the-truth	sannundum
the-Wise	snielli
they	þa, þaar, þaim, þair, þaira, þairi, þann, þar, þau, þaun, þet, þy
think	hyggia
third	þriþi, þriþia, þriþiung, þriþiunga, þriþiungi, þriþiungr
thirds	þriþiunga
this	hitta, þa, þann, Þet, þinna, þissi, þissum, þissun, þitta
though	þau
thought	hugþi, þytti
three	þria, þriar, þrim, þrir, þriþi, þriþiung, þriþiunga, þriþiungi, þriþiungr, þry
through	ginum, um
thus	so, þinna
time	bragþ, bragþi, frest, frestum, tima, timi
Tjelvar	Þieluar
Tjelvar (a name)	Þieluar
to	a, at, hugþi, i, innan, til, viþr
together	bundit, saman
together with	miþ
told	segþi
tolerate	þula
toll	tuldr, tull
to-me	mir
took	tok, toki, Toku
Torsburgen	Þorsborg
Torsburgen (a place)	Þorsborg
to-take	taka
to-them	þaim
touch	royra
towards	viþr
town	kaupungr
trading	kaupmannaskap, kaup-mannaskap, kaupmannaskepr
trading voyages	kaupmannaskap, kaup-mannaskap, kaupmannaskepr
trading-man	kaupmaþr
trading-men	kaupmenn
trading-voyages	kaup-mannaskap

Word List (English to Old Gutnish)

English	Old Gutnish
traing town	kaupungr
travel	fara, fari, farit, ferþar, for, fori, foru, sykia
travelled	fara, for, fori, foru
travelling	fara
travel-to	sykia
treaty	ret, retr, retum
tribute	gingerþ, gingerþa, siþ, siþi, siþir, siþr, skatt, skattr
trip	ferd, ferþ
truth	sannund, sannundum
tumulus	hauga, haugr
twelve	tolf
twenty	tiughu, tiugu
two	tu, tua, tuair, tvair, tvar

U, u

English	Old Gutnish
unborn	ofydum
unburnt	obrend
un-burnt	obrend
unconsecrated	ovigþ
undedicated	ovigþ
under	undir
undertake	taka, taki, tok, toki, toku
undertaking	skap, skepr
unfortunate	illa
unfortunately	illa
unhindered	frels, frelsir
united	bundit
unlawful	olaglika
un-law-like	olaglika
unless	utan
until	til
up	upp, uppi
upp	upp
Uppsala	Upsala

V, v

English	Old Gutnish
valuable	klenat, klenatum
valuables	klenatum
versatile	fielkunnugr
Vi	Vi
victory	sigr, sigri
village	socn
Visby	Vi
visible	synas, synis
visit	sykia, tilquemd, tilquemda
visitation	tilquemd, tilquemda
voyage	ferþ, ferþar

W, w

English	Old Gutnish
wait	biþa
wait for	biþa
Walburga	Valborga
Walburga (a place)	Valborga
waning (of the moon)	niþ, niþar
waning-moon	niþar
want	vil, vildi, vildu, vili, vilia, viliandi, vilin
war	her
war-army	her
war-gold	vereldi
war-journey	herferþ
warship	snekkia, snekkiu, snekkium
warships	snekkium
war-travel	herferþ
war-voyage	herferþ
was	ir, var, varþ
was-called	kallar
water	vatn, vatni
watercourse	vatn, vatni
waxing	ny
waxing moon	ny
waxing-moon	ny
way	vegin, vegr
we	uir, vir
wedding	bryþlaupr
week	vika, vikna, viku, wica
weeks'	vikna
weight of silver	oyri, oyrum
well	uel, vel
were	varin, varu

Word List (English to Old Gutnish) — Orþalisti

English	Old Gutnish
wergild	vereldi
wergilds	vereldi
what	huat, hut
when	en, þa
which	sum, þa, þaar, þaim, þair, þaira, þairi, þann, þar, þaun, þet, þy
while	miþan
white	huit
White Star (a name)	Huitastierna
White-Star	Huitastierna
who	sum
whole	aldr, aldra, all, alla, allan, allar, allir, allum, alt
widow	enkia
wife	froyia, husfroyu, kuna, kunu
will	al, skal, skuldi, skuldin, skuldu, skulin, skulu, vil, vildi, vildu, vili, vilia, viliandi, vilin
willed	vildi
willing	vil, vildi, vildu, vili, vilia, viliandi, vilin
willingly	viliandi
wind	byr, byriar
winter	vittr
winter-time	vintrtima, vintrtimi, vittr
wise	Snelli, Snieldr, Snielli
wish	vil, vildi, vildu, vili, vilia, viliandi, vilin
wished	vildi
with	at, meþ, miþ, viþr
within	hugþi, i
without	laus, utan
without blame	saklausu
without charge	saklaus
without fine	saklaus
without obligation	saklaus
woman	cuna, husfroyia, husfroyu
womb	barmbr, barmi
work	arfuþi
world	vereld
would	vildi
wound	sar
write	scrifa

Y, y

English	Old Gutnish
yard	garþi, garþr, karþr
yarn	garn
Yaroslav	Ierslafs
year	ar, ari, huert, vittr
yearling (a year old animal)	veþru, veþur
years	ar
you	ir, þu
you (plural)	ir
young	ungr
youngest	yngsti

www.ingramcontent.com/pod-product-compliance
Lightning Source LLC
Chambersburg PA
CBHW051424070526
44584CB00023B/3575